HUMAN SECURITY

Human Security

SOME REFLECTIONS

W. E. BLATZ

University of Toronto Press

© *University of Toronto Press 1966*
Reprinted 1967, 2014
ISBN 978-1-4426-5203-3 (paper)

To my grandsons
JEFFREY and *JIMMY*

Foreword • D. C. WILLIAMS

DR. WILLIAM BLATZ was the founder of the nursery school movement in Canada. His St. George's School which opened in 1925 as an adjunct to the Psychology Department at the University of Toronto, was one of the first of its kind in North America. By 1938 the University formally recognized its essential nature and made it the Institute of Child Study. Together with the Banting Institute (1930), it served Toronto in a unique capacity for many years.

Dr. Blatz was thus one of the pioneers of the institute idea. He encouraged interdisciplinary study not only because the many facets of child life demanded it, but also because he himself had integrated the disciplines of medicine and psychology in his own experience by taking doctoral degrees in both.

Today we accept as commonplace the idea of the institute or centre as an interdisciplinary body designed to bring scholars of different backgrounds together for research on problems of mutual interest. But it was not always so. Like all good academic ideas, this one first had to win its way against the opposition of those who saw all academic virtue encapsulated in the idea of the university department. The Institute of Child Study is important, then, not only in its own right, but also as an early and excellent example of the institute idea, an encouragement to others to undertake interdisciplinary studies.

This is a significant part of Dr. Blatz's legacy to the University of Toronto. Another and related part of that legacy is to be found in his theory of personality, expounded in this book. The theory, elaborated and revised over a lifetime, and profoundly influenced by his work in the Institute of Child Study, is his attempt to "see [psychological] life steadily and see it whole." To a great extent Dr. Blatz *was* his theory, a fact which enabled him to communicate it effectively to others, many of whom became deeply persuaded of its merits. A generation of graduate students found it a stimulating and fruitful source of hypotheses for research, and a host of parents, parent educators, nursery-school workers, and clinicians found in it an illuminating aid in understanding personality development. One can wish that the book had been written earlier, but the fact is that Dr. Blatz waited until his retirement to find time to write it. To some readers its language will sound old-fashioned and so will some of its ideas. These drawbacks are a small price to pay for its honesty, its clarity, and its insight into some of the vexing problems of living and learning.

One word of warning. "Security Theory," to use the common graduate-student nickname, is not to be confused with safety; indeed these two ideas turn out to be virtually antithetical. He who merely seeks safety can never be secure. But here I begin to trespass on the domain of the author, who is fully capable of speaking for himself.

Preface • MARY L. NORTHWAY

W. E. BLATZ was primarily and consistently a teacher. He taught, not to instruct, but to provoke. This he succeeded in doing, whether he was lecturing to undergraduates, supervising graduate seminars, talking to home and school clubs, giving after-dinner speeches, or appearing on television. His lectures became a dialogue between himself and his audience. He stimulated thought, while his listeners responded by silently but actively contradicting his statements, supporting his thesis extending his examples, interpreting or misinterpreting his implications, rebutting his arguments, and appreciating or depreciating his wit. True to his own educational philosophy, that it is what is learned that matters, not what is taught, he encouraged continual effort in his listeners, so that they eagerly awaited the end of the lecture for an opportunity to "talk back" audibly and express ideas of their own which they considered were better, sounder, more logical, more scientific, more rational, and often more conventional than his. Rarely did such opportunity come, however, for the lecturer would slip quickly and unobtrusively out of the room, leaving his listeners to argue among themselves and learn from one another.

To produce the active listener, Blatz effectively and perhaps deliberately employed two devices. One was the use of overstatement which was easy for the listener to correct, contradict, or deny; the other device was to leave the argument, example, or reference at loose ends with a large "etcetera." This technique incited the listener to continue, complete, or clarify the matter by his own efforts. "It is not what the teacher says that is important, it is what it inspires his pupils to go ahead and do." Blatz provoked not merely reaction but action; the repercussions of the lecture continued long after the class was dismissed.

This book may be considered one more lecture series. The listener, now the reader, will be provoked. He cannot help becoming active. He may be irritated, challenged, baffled, enthralled, or inspired. He will not be simply indifferent, nor will he be bored. He may dismiss ideas as old fashioned, unscientific, or illogical, in which case he will have to provide himself with better ones, or he may say, "That's exactly what I always thought," in which case he will have to admit that the writer is at least as wise as he is. He will find the same devices used herein: overstatements which he will wish to challenge; loose ends from which he can complete the argument or to which he can add illustrations from his own life experience and wisdom.

Blatz talked, studied, investigated, and lectured the theory of Security for the last twenty-five years of his life, and was continually "about to write a book on it." As he implies in his own introduction, the theory was not derived from specific sources or constructed solely from the findings of scientific investigations; rather it grew from a lifetime of experiences, both broad and deep, covering the gamut of professional activities of a psychologist: research, teaching, counselling, child guidance, parent education, and university administration. But his experiences expanded far beyond these conventional areas into the wide world of a human being who loved life richly and perceived all aspects of it as valid psychological evidence. Thus as Blatz grew, his theory grew. Readers who are familiar with his earlier statements will find them considerably modified here. Instead of his earlier ideal of the independent man, there is much more emphasis on the importance of both immature and mature dependency. This may be due to his interest in the evidence coming from the infant, pre-school, and social studies carried out by his staff over the last fifteen years. Or it may be that through the illness and increasing frailty of the last nine years of his life, he discovered personally the necessity and joy of mature dependency and learned that to be independent was not enough in itself.

It should be noted that this book was written after Blatz's retirement. Away from the frets and frays of his battleground, he reflected on the experiences of a long and busy lifetime and selected those which remained of greatest significance. All of what he had to say about the security theory is not included, but what he finally considered worth saying is distilled here. We have therefore given the book the title, *Human Security: Some Reflections.* In view of Blatz's theory of consciousness, the term "reflections" seems particularly appropriate. A usage of the word dating back to 1690 is recorded thus in the Oxford Dictionary: "The mode, operation or faculty by which the mind has knowledge of itself and its operations, or by which it deals with the ideas received from sensation and perception."

Blatz always loved an audience, even an audience of one. He hated and was somewhat frightened by mechanical aids. After his retirement from the Institute of Child Study he invited me to go to his home for a morning a week both to serve as his audience and to run the tape recorder. As an audience I was valuable as a sounding board, perhaps because during the years I was on his staff I had never been involved in his security studies, and had continually disputed many of the fundamentals of his theory. As tape recorderist I offered no threat, as I was able to deal with the apparatus only slightly less ineptly than he. We found we had often lost some of the most puckish passages, or superimposed three themes on one record, resulting in the transcription of complete gibberish. Blatz would dictate for about half an hour and then say, "Turn that dingus off. How did that sound? Now tell me, what do you think?"

And I would reply, "It was very clear, but in this day and age you simply can't say that 'all social patterns in the human being are learned.' Recent evidence shows . . ."

"Well that doesn't matter; remember, in my theory all social behaviour is a device a person uses to get what he wants. This is what I have come to believe from the evidence of a lifetime. So I can say so if I want."

Two psychologists who have subsequently read the manuscript have both exclaimed, "He can't say that! In this day and age to vilify the unconscious and to advocate the use of introspection is impossible." But the tape recorder is at OFF, and such objections have not entered the manuscript. It is probable that each reader will interject at some point, "But he can't say that": "Boredom is the source of independent effort," or "An individual has only one or two friends in a lifetime."

But Blatz would answer, "Indeed I can. Not because it is based on research or found in the books, but because from my knowledge and experience it is what I think. The only thing we can finally trust is our own experience out of which that which we call our wisdom has grown." And then he would add to me, "Remember, it's I who have to accept the consequences of what I say, if we ever get it finished so there'll be some consequences. Turn on that dingus."

Following these tape-recording sessions, Blatz rewrote most of the manuscript by hand. In October 1964 he considered it so close to completion that he arranged a meeting for early November with Miss

Halpenny of the University of Toronto Press and myself to begin preparation for publication. He had often mentioned his wish that Professor William Line and Professor Bruce Quarrington would read it before it went to press. However, Dr. Line's untimely death in the spring of 1964 prevented his giving us advice which we all would have appreciated. Following Blatz's sudden death in November, 1964, Dr. Quarrington and I, with Miss Halpenny's advice, went straight ahead with our duties.

I have attempted to have it come out exactly as it would have if Blatz had had the opportunity to say the last word. It had been suggested that Chapter 2 on Consciousness might be better placed at the end of the manuscript. I mentioned this to Blatz when I read an earlier draft some two years ago. His answer was, "No, it has to come at the beginning—it's essential to my system. But we can tell the reader to skip it and begin at Chapter 3." For a time we considered the suggestion that an introduction should be written setting the security theory in the current perspective of modern psychology and commenting on it as an expression of an existential and rational philosophy. But on reflection we decided that W. E. Blatz had never needed an apologia and had always been capable of defending himself. To interpret him in his own book would be no compliment, for he often maintained, as he stated more formally in his own introduction, "There will be no references or footnotes. Those who know psychology will recognize where I have borrowed, those that don't, don't care."

I have done little to change the manuscript. Many of the "etc.'s" the author left have been removed in conformity with literary custom. Paragraphs have been re-ordered to give continuity to the argument— a continuity Blatz obtained in his lectures by the use of his well-loved blackboard. However, the reader is still left with the task of effecting his own closure. Each will do so in his own way, so the results will be different and the interpretations many. I have added a brief postscript stating the recurring questions that the theory aroused, and Blatz's answers to them. I have also included a list of the studies and publications which have been derived from Blatz's Security Theory. Two of these may be considered companion pieces that illuminate and extend this book: Dr. Mary Ainsworth's scholarly interpretation of the studies of adult security, *The Security of Personal Adjustment*, and Professor Betty Flint's developmental investigations, *The Security of Infants*.

Blatz's most recent book, *Understanding the Young Child*, appeared twenty-one years ago. It contained one chapter on security. He was often asked why he had not published more on his theory himself, and he was sometimes criticized for failing to do so. I asked him about this in one of our tape-recording sessions when the "dingus" was at OFF. His reply may be paraphrased thus: "During my lifetime I have tried to do two things—develop a theory and build an Institute. In 1950 I had to make a choice whether to continue putting my efforts into lecturing and writing and going to conferences—and remember, I was never one of the publish-or-perish coterie—or whether to use these efforts towards building up a school in which long-term studies of development could be made, and creating a staff competent to continue such studies. As you know, I chose the latter course and spent endless time persuading the authorities, collecting funds, reconstructing the buildings, and submitting reports to our grantors. So what have I achieved? Not wide recognition for my theory, although in these days when everybody spells publication with a capital "P" this might have been the more approved choice. But rather we have a unique school, an understanding and increasingly productive staff, high acceptance by the community, especially in education and mental health, and a great many friends who support our goal. Since I believe the future will see the results of this effort, I am quite willing to accept the consequences of my decision."

Dr. Blatz would want acknowledgment made to his many colleagues and students who have listened to, discussed, strengthened, derided, and criticized the Security Theory. He was also grateful to Mrs. Marie Davis, Mrs. Irma Ross, and Mrs. Jill Oman, who typed earlier versions of the material. I would add my own appreciation to Professors Quarrington, Millichamp, and Ainsworth, whom I have consulted on parts of the manuscript; however, the final revision is wholly my responsibility. Further acknowledments are due to Mrs. Felicia Atkinson, Mrs. Clara Kovrig, Mrs. Clare Denaburg, and Miss Jean Quinn, who have speeded the typing of the final copies; to Miss Francess Halpenny and Mr. Jan Schreiber of the University of Toronto Press, who have been helpful with editorial advice; to Dr. Carl Williams, Blatz's former student, colleague, and friend, who has taken time from his duties as Vice-President of the University to write the Foreword; to the W. E. Blatz Memorial Fund for Publications, for a small grant made to expedite publication of this book; and most particularly to Mrs. W. E. Blatz and Mrs. Margery de Roux who asked me to complete the manuscript and had confidence that I would see it through to publication.

Institute of Child Study
August, 1965 *University of Toronto*

Contents

HUMAN SECURITY

1 · Introduction

THE ANCIENTS had a word for it, *cacoethes scribendi*, the urge to write. And so after fifty years of more or less formal observation of the most fascinating objects in the world around us, namely other human beings, I feel impelled to put on paper what I think I have learned and the circumstances under which such learning took place.

In such an introduction, the personal pronoun is not out of place. Self-conceit in its original context meant a good opinion of one's self. Provided it is not wholly unjustified, it is not indictable. With this risk in mind, I will, here, give a brief chronology of the events which led up to the writing of this book. Herein I have stated a theory of human development. I have been fortunate enough to have had the opportunity of testing its reliability and validity in the research, clinical, and educational settings. It has been found not altogether wanting.

I obtained a B.A. in 1916 and a master's degree in Physiology in 1917 at the University of Toronto. The thesis was on a study on the adrenal glands. This was in the middle of World War I. I found the authorities perhaps justifiably reluctant to accept me as a combatant because, although I was a Canadian by birth, I was one of a German family. My parents came to Canada nearly one hundred years ago. My father, Leo, had left Wurzburg in 1868, while my mother Victoria Mesmer, who was related to Franz Anton Mesmer, of animal magnetism fame, came from Mainz a couple of years later. They were married in Hamilton, Ontario, in 1871. My father was a craftsman in glazing bricks. Later, he became established as a tailor. (I have his original scissors.) Meanwhile, my mother produced nine children, of whom I, born in 1895, was the youngest.

After having been rejected from the services I met, by chance, a man who was to have a large part in my future career, Professor

E. A. Bott, a psychologist on the staff of the University of Toronto. Through his own efforts he had organized a group of volunteers to help in the care of some of the wounded Canadian soldiers already returned from France. These patients were mostly chronic cases with some psychological involvement; nerve injuries, so-called shell shock, and amputations. With great ingenuity he had devised gadgets to deal with such patients and so provide a means of motivating them to try to help themselves. He asked me to join his group. I did so and became part of the Hart House re-education team.

Shortly afterwards this enterprise was incorporated into the Royal Canadian Army Medical Corps, and I found myself a staff sergeant in a military hospital nominally in charge of research in the field of mental illness.

Although the successful results were gratifying, the failures were disappointing and baffling. The literature of the day was not illuminating, especially in the field of psychology. I learned that *in our work we were dealing with a phenomenon more elusive than any other— consciousness.* (Of course later on I learned that I wasn't the first to discover any of these matters, but I am reporting as *I* learned them.)

I decided then that this was to be the area of my vocation.

The war was over! I was back at the University of Toronto Medical School to finish the last year of my clinical work, to become manager of the Varsity football team that won the Grey Cup in 1920, and to obtain my M.B. in 1921. Included in my clinical year there were four lectures in Psychiatry, none in Psychology, and one demonstration of a patient who thought she was Queen Victoria. Thus my decision was strengthened to find out exactly what psychology had to offer in the understanding of human beings.

Sponsored by Bott I was awarded a scholarship (it just paid my fees) in the Department of Psychology at the University of Chicago. There I met one of my best teachers, and later a genial and congenial colleague, Professor Harvey Carr. There I studied and taught at a time when psychology was just emerging from a rather sterile sojourn in the laboratory into the field of total human behaviour. I learned that:

The studies of mental activities, e.g. memory, attention, sensation, and perception were being interpreted in the light of their contribution to total behaviour rather than as separate and isolated faculties.

It is easy to take the results of statistical analysis too seriously.

Examinations of adults, if there is no knowledge of the beginnings of mental development, leave a great deal to be desired.

A great deal can be learned from an examination of children.

Others were thinking in the same direction. Almost overnight "the young child" was discovered. In medicine, dentistry, education, nutrition, and other related fields, the interest of the research student was aroused.

In 1924 I received my Ph.D. from Chicago, my thesis being on a study of physiological changes produced by emotion. At this time, the Department of Psychology at the University of Toronto was given a grant by the Laura Spelman Rockefeller Memorial Foundation for the study of the mental and social development of young children, under the supervision of Dr. C. M. Hincks and Professor E. A. Bott. I was given the opportunity to join the group which was gathered together to conduct this enterprise. And so the St. George's Nursery School was founded, later to become the Institute of Child Study.

The story of the growth of the Institute has been told elsewhere, in the book by the staff presented to me on my twenty-fifth year as director, entitled *Twenty-Five Years of Child Study*, and in the Institute's other publications. From the original school for eight children, it had grown until at the time of my retirement, it comprised a nursery and elementary school for 150 children, a parent education and student teaching division, and a research staff which maintained what I had visualized in the beginning—a programme of longitudinal study of the development of the children in our schools. This research was the central core of the Institute, in spite of its many difficulties and vicissitudes.

During these years the Institute was my base. I remained as its Director until 1960 and continued as Professor of Psychology until 1963. There in the early days I learned that:

Very young children have no imagination. They have images. They are realists and credulous. The apparent imaginative powers lie in the adult interpretation of their mistakes in dealing with their world— inner and outer. Curiosity, however, is an inherent pattern that must be fostered to prevent its disuse. Children are far less complex than adults, a fact which assists the observer in his interpretations, provided he does not use adult patterns as his guide.

The Nursery School procedure which proves most effective is one composed of a wide area of permissiveness surrounded by a consistent control.

Self-destruction and unwarranted interference with others must be prevented.

Children are happier when a schedule is provided for their guidance, but the schedule must be minimal and consistent.

Understanding a child's needs permits a good teacher to anticipate wants and hence to satisfy the child or redirect him.

Punishment in the Old Testament sense is contra-indicated.

Retaliation always breeds violence.

So I stayed at the University of Toronto until I retired in 1963. It is not at present fashionable to stay in one place so long; it is considered stagnating. I considered it essential to follow the process of these children's development. The statistical method of sampling at succeeding ages gave rapid results, but the individual was often lost in the shuffle. I also managed to overcome stagnation by lecturing at universities from Moscow to Honolulu, from Florida to Santiago, from Halifax to Vancouver, from Vermont to San Francisco.

Shortly after the founding of the Nursery School, I was appointed Psychological Consultant to the Juvenile Court of Toronto and in close association with the late Dr. G. Anderson was given the opportunity of studying the so-called delinquent child. In my court work I learned that:

Delinquency is a matter of definition; statistics in this field are more often unreliable and invalid than they appear.

Children make mistakes and the total eradication of these mistakes is impossible.

The basic condition of so-called delinquents is "boredom." Violence is often the result of, rather than the cause for, the anti-social behaviour.

The job of the court is to prevent adult *delinquency, which does not necessarily arise directly out of its juvenile counterpart.*

At the same time a research plan for observing the so-called normal school child (the ones who weren't caught) was put under way, and for five years a team established by Dr. C. M. Hincks was able to work closely with the school-age child at the Regal Road Public School, Toronto. This was the first time psychological study had been carried out in a public school of this city. In our studies at Regal Road I learned that:

School-age "problems" arise from uninspiring teachers, unimaginative curricula, and rigid standards of progress. Superimposed on this quagmire is an astonishing intellectual snobbishness which had its beginning in the Middle Ages and is currently fostered by the spread of misinformation about the "intelligence" test, which has become a dangerous tool in the hands of the amateur.

All knowledge is useful only if it is used. How it is used is another matter. Unused knowledge does not lie fallow like a field "resting"; it just disappears.

In the thirties I had placed our graduate students in two of the agencies for the care of neglected and/or deserted children—the Children's Aid Society and the Infants' Home. "Clinics" were established under our supervision until they were wholly incorporated into the institutional staff roster. I learned that:

Early care of the infant is most important in establishing a secure basis for later experience.

This care should not be interrupted too frequently by change in the persons who are caring for the child.

The most convenient and adequate "agent" for this care is the child's mother—but not because she is the mother, rather because of other attributes which can readily be supplied by another.

"Love" is the most ambiguous word in the English lexicon, especially when applied to the child-adult relationship. Parental love, especially mother love, is presumed to make allowance for all sorts of shortcomings in child care. Even today the most atrocious incidents of cruelty to their children by parents are held rather lightly by our courts.

Consistency is the most important quality in guiding a child. Sincere affection can compensate for inevitable lapses in operation, but "love" without consistency is a dangerous indulgence.

In the early thirties I became Director of the Windy Ridge Day School. This was a school for children two to eight years of age, which was run by its own board of professional men and women. It continued until 1953, when it was combined with St. George's. Here I enjoyed meeting many non-university people and I learned that these non-academics could think equally well and were far less convention-bound and more genuinely concerned about seeking knowledge of children than were many of my university colleagues.

During this period, psychology in universities, business, and everyday life both amateur and professional flourished like the Green Bay Tree. The subject began to increase in importance. Departments of psychology were emancipated from their parental philosophy roots. Courses were given hither and yon and more significantly invaded the medical curricula. I was given the opportunity of delivering lectures in "Mental Hygiene" to second year students; I also conducted a seminar for graduates in psychiatry and an out-patient clinic at the Psychiatric Hospital, which medical students attended. I learned more than my students—that:

Mental illness is often self-limiting.
Unnecessary restraint usually aggravates or prolongs the condition.
The adult condition resembles the behaviour of a recalcitrant child.
Patients often come too late for treatment of conditions which should have been prevented.

In the·early days of this century the Health Service at the University of Toronto was primarily concerned with physical examination of athletes: Later this service was extended to all undergraduates, male and female. Then an infirmary was set up for emergency treatment. The staff increased in numbers and efficiency. Mental problems in these early years were ignored or referred to hospitals, but gradually a few of the deans would refer a student to the informal service at the Institute. In this way I became familiar with some of the perennial problems of adolescence: examinationitis, status frustrations, religious confusion, sexual indiscretions and bafflement, evangelistic fervours, etc. I learned over the years that:

Adolescence is not necessarily a period of "Sturm und Drang" but has a place in normal development that provides no more conflicts than any other period of development.
It is in the solving of adolescent conflicts that the outbursts arise.
With adequate early preparation and experience of solving problems, adolescence can be "taken" with the same success and aplomb as any other growth phenomenon.

In the middle thirties a rather dramatic interlude in my programme of learning occurred. It was initiated by the startling news that a mother in Northern Ontario had given birth to five daughters at one time: the soon famous Dionne quintuplets! Elsewhere the story has been told of our association with Professors Norma Ford Walker and J. A. McArthur in studies of these identical sisters. I learned from them that:

The growth of the intelligence is largely due to an inherited factor.
Personality is largely a matter of social patterns. It is acquired and only incidentally inborn.

In the forties, the Second World War brought many changes. At the request of the Ministry of Health of Great Britain, and spurred again by the organizing energy of Clare Hincks, I took a team of Canadian nursery workers to Birmingham where we developed the Garrison Lane Nursery which became a training demonstration centre for nursery workers throughout the country. There I learned, among other things, that:

Children have amazing powers of resilience.
Consistent care is more important than maternal care.
People have great courage when pressing for a principle.

Meanwhile on the home front, with a small staff left to man the Institute, day nurseries and nursery schools grew like mushrooms to meet the needs of mothers in industry. Our staff gave all kinds of courses to women going into the nursery profession, and in 1946 we established a full year's course for graduate students leading to a Diploma in Child Study. It was the first officially recognized course in this area in a Canadian university. At the same time, we worked on standards and regulations for nurseries which later became incorporated into an official act of the Ontario Government. Soon nursery associations were formed, and at the opening dinner of the Nursery Education Association of Ontario, I found myself referred to as "the grandfather of the nursery school movement."

From this I learned that a loyal staff could carry on and expand activities while I was away. And also:

Bad nurseries are worse than none, for children's mental health suffers in an improperly controlled group, and children are the easiest things to exploit unless they are legally protected.
Ideas that lie fallow, given opportune circumstances, eventually germinate.

During the late forties my work at the Family Court was largely occupied with the increasing number of couples who came for advice (usually too late) concerning marital discord of some kind. From this experience I learned that:

The concept that a "broken home" implies only that one or the other parent is missing is naive.
The so-called sex traumata of the early Freudian school are relatively insignificant in their effect on children.
An understanding of the disciplinary plan is the most important activity for diagnosing the source of family difficulty.
In our Western civilization more problems are concerned with the

*handling of the family income, large or small, than with any other
aspect of family life.*

Boredom looms large as a precipitating factor.

After the war came the days of the bulge in student teaching. In
the late forties we gathered a group of graduate students at the Institute to study various aspects of the theory I had gradually developed
of Human Security. This had been first described by my student and
colleague, Dr. Mary Ainsworth, in her monograph on *The Concept of
Security* in 1940. I included a chapter on it in my book *Understanding
the Young Child*, in 1944. For these studies, grants were obtained from
the Defence Research Board and some fifteen theses were written,
later to be followed by a number of books. From the study programme
I learned three things: that the security theory which provoked interest and enthusiasm could, in spite of difficulties, be submitted to
research; that I could learn much from my students; that to complete
our investigations would require half a century and an observational
school where we could study children at least as far as adolescence.

In the fifties the Institute grew. I had plans drawn up for a new
school and research facilities to be built near the main campus of the
university. The plans were unacceptable to the authorities of the time,
but we were given a house some distance away, which had been
bequeathed to the University by Leighton McCarthey. Here I combined Windy Ridge and the St. Georges School and each year added
grades up to VI. To obtain sufficient space I canvassed my friends
for the funds to build a new school wing and to remodel the three-car
garage into experimental rooms.

From 1953 to 1958 we were financed for the most part with funds
from the National Department of Health and Welfare for research
into the development of mental health. These funds paid all our staff
salaries. Each year we submitted reports of our progress.

In 1958 the University of Toronto sent in an investigating commit-
tee, and after its report to the authorities, the Board of Governors
decided to pick up the tab on our total budget. So we became by no
means the smallest faculty in the University, and I felt that the future
of our years of effort was now secured. From these years I learned
that:

Administration is often a wasteful and thankless effort.

Good effort is increasingly in danger of being strangled by red tape.

*A staff not only clarifies a director's ideas, but can take the initiative
in developing them in new directions.*

It is when children become nine or so that one begins to see the results of a training plan. Their values, "code," and judgment crystallize around them.

In the fifties too, there was an awakened interest in the unusual child, the retarded, the gifted, the crippled, the cerebral palsied and others, as well as a renewed and concentrated attack on physical illnesses. The brilliant and successful attack on polio gave an impetus to research in child welfare. In the mental area, a hospital for the care and study of disturbed children was founded in Ontario. I was given the opportunity of working closely with Dr. Donald Atcheson, the Superintendent, in the arranging of the educational programme. I learned (after I had wondered where all these children had been when I first entered this field 40 years ago) that:

Disturbed children differ from so-called normal children in their emphasis upon certain behaviour patterns and in their outlook on life.

Comparison of this group with a school group of comparable age and intelligence shows a striking similarity in qualitative but not quantitative patterns.

Emotional tantrums of disturbed children are similar to those in young normal children or adults, but they differ in intensity, complexity, and duration. The treatment, however, is the same.

From the beginning of the Toronto project in Child Study, teaching was recognized to be as important as the research programme. Formal education, especially in the lower grades, has always presented a paradox. Whereas the textbooks have usually been ten years behind times, some of the teaching has reached far into the future. A great deal depended on the teacher. From Genesis to Einstein what was taught in the classroom was presumed to be the truth. From time to time truth was brought up to date. This arrangement is inevitable. If one waited for a final truth, there would be no teaching at all.

And so we organized, in the early days, a Parent Education Division. Through it we tried to interpret conclusions drawn from the investigations and pass them on to the parents, who tried to apply them to their "needs" of the moment. They were bringing up their children and couldn't wait for the "final way." This presented a novel experience for some of us. For most teachers, both in the elementary schools and in the higher echelons, there was usually a time lag between the lecture and the application of the content in actual living. In Parent Education the matter was discussed and conclusions

drawn in the morning and perhaps applied that afternoon! No wonder
that in the early days the procedures recommended were usually
"rule of thumb" palliatives! Every year the plan of study was scruti-
nized and adapted to new knowledge. The efficacy of the teaching as
well as an evaluation of the material used in the classes provided a
fruitful source for research. I learned that:

*Parent education is the most effective plan for putting into practice
a programme of positive mental health.*

Prevention is less costly than cure—and not only in money.

*There will never be enough experts (psychologists, psychiatrists,
social workers, etc.) to treat problems.*

*There are two groups which come into contact with all children
over a sufficient period of time to make an effective impact—parents
and teachers—but only if they are adequately prepared for the job.
There are thus two educational tasks: (1) teach the teachers; (2) teach
the parents; and there is one further important job—research—to find
out more and more about children, and hence adults.*

Gradually the need for a unifying principle to embrace what I was
learning made itself felt. The use of the "unconscious" as an explanatory scapegoat for all kinds of behaviour was unsatisfactory. The
growing tendency on the part of the individual to shout "Give me
liberty or give me death," and then in the next breath to demand
more assistance, protection, and subsidies from the "government" was
baffling to say the least. The results of my learning began to point in
one direction. A central guiding principle should have these definite
qualifications:

*It must refer to a positive aspect of health, not just the absence of
disease.*

*It must have an objective character so that it can be observed, de-
scribed, and hence be available for research.*

It must have a conscious aspect.

It must be operative from birth to death.

It must apply to all living organisms.

It must explain both normal and abnormal conditions.

*It must restore to human experience the concept of "responsibility"
as the only avenue for the acquisition of personal dignity.*

During the early thirties such a principle began to take form in my
thinking. Resisting the temptation to give it a Greek name I called it
security and defined it as follows.

Security is the state of mind which accompanies the willingness to accept the consequences of one's acts—without equivocation of any sort. The feeling accompanying this state may be called *serenity*. Security is the basic goal of all living beings.

Achievement of this goal would indicate complete mental health. Any departure from this achievement indicates the degree of mental ill health. Such departures would imply some form of "passing the buck"—the most common form of human behaviour—to avoid responsibility and acquire a dependence on something or someone.

To accept responsibility is to be independent of anything but oneself—thus to seek safety is not a secure pattern but rather implies insecurity.

This book is written to describe the development of security patterns in human beings. It is divided into theory and implications. Chapters 2 to 10 describe the theory as completely as possible. Chapter 11 outlines the implication of the theory for various aspects of mental health.

The chapter on consciousness forms the basis of the subsequent argument. However, it can be skipped without interfering too much with an understanding of the theory. A few graphs are included. These are not statistical. They are attempts to make the text easier to understand rather than to confuse the reader. They are not necessarily accurate in detail.

Although the child looms large in the illustrations and examples, since we all begin as children, it is assumed that the content as a whole applies also to adults.

The reader will find no footnotes, no references, in fact, nothing but the text to attract his attention. This is not presumptuousness on my part. Anyone familiar with the psychological field will recognize at once where I have "borrowed" from others. To those unfamiliar with developmental psychology it will not matter.

I have tried throughout to avoid awkward and unfamiliar terms and as far as possible to avoid introducing a new vocabulary. Wherever a new term was necessary, I have used an English word and then by careful definition tried to give it a precise meaning in the text. However, the study of human everyday life is so close to all of us that a term first used in a meaningful manner is taken up and used in ordinary speech so frequently and inappropriately that it often loses its original usefulness—for example, "image" is a much abused term. At any rate this shows that people are interested in the subject.

For anything original in this presentation I take full responsibility.

2 · Consciousness

In which we encounter a rather tedious discussion of consciousness; of the senses and paying attention; of striving and the origin of wants; of meanings; of feelings: pleasant and unpleasant wants; of moments of consciousness and how they smooth out to appear continuous; of recall, memory, and forgetting; of the reactor system; of projecting consciousness apparently into the future; of images and concepts.

MOST PEOPLE are fairly healthy physically although there are very few who have absolutely nothing wrong with them; it may be only a hangnail. Similarly most people are fairly well mentally although there are very, very few who at times do not show some signs of distress. Indeed, most people carry on physically or mentally without undue interruptions, in spite of intermittant inadequacies. There are two sides to the picture of mental health: how the person appears to other people, and how he inwardly feels himself. There is a great deal of unalloyed misery in the world that no one hears about. It is locked up inside people who seldom confide in anyone. There are the more dramatic pictures of the maniacs, the suicides, the vandals, and the destroyers. These are the extreme examples of the misfits. Fortunately there are not a great number of these in the world. Their episodes of unnatural behaviour are still "news." *Perhaps* heredity has something to do with some of these.

But in the great majority of people there are prejudices that encircle and embitter their lives, meannesses that make social life a contentious miserable existence, blasted ambitions that sear the soul, jealousies that curdle the blood, obstinate principles that make friendship impossible, fanaticism, bigotry, vengeance, and all the inner tortures of the mind. These are not hereditary. These patterns of behaviour are *learned*. They are the amalgam of all the influences that have had an inevitable impact on the individual personality.

Workers in mental health are interested not only in preventing these, but in promoting positive qualities—co-operation, charity, kindliness, consideration, fulfilled dreams, and concrete achievement. These too are not inherited. The destiny of an individual is in his own hands, or so we believe.

All of this is nebulous. It is a twice-told tale. Everyone will agree that it would be a better world if we all helped each other, avoided quarrels, extended mercy, gave up bitterness, and were never jealous; but, they ask, "How is this to be accomplished?"

Here is my answer:

A person who is mentally healthy must not only act as such; he must feel as such. *When a person is willing to accept the consequences of his actions, he is healthy, and when he is acting in this fashion, he feels healthy. Such an individual is said to be secure and to feel serene.* His mental life is devoted to achieving this harmony. Whether he succeeds or not is incidental. The important thing is that he is at least continually *trying* to attain security and enjoy serenity. This is the thesis which I will describe and then defend in this book.

A healthy mental state may be described as that which accompanies a person's willingness to accept the consequences of his decisions and hence actions, no matter what they may be. In such a state the individual feels serene. He is not tempted to use any of the anti-social behaviour patterns or ideas mentioned above, but will find the acceptable patterns of living more effective.

People are interesting! They may be fascinating, loathesome, beautiful, hideous, dull, brilliant, endearing, or repulsive, but all are interesting. None more so than ourselves. We tick!

One of our most interesting activities is our curiosity. Each one of us is, at times, our own doctor, cook, raconteur, entertainer, artist, and in these days especially, psychologist. Only the very shy person avoids an opportunity to expound his own theory of the cause and cure of delinquency, divorce, alcoholism, crime, unemployment, and particularly the vagaries of sex. In attempts at explanation the most fashionable theory of the day is unwittingly plagiarized, often with gracious acknowledgment to the author who would shudder at the casual misinterpretation.

Almost everybody today believes in the unconscious. Although no one has seen it, examined it directly, or heard any real evidence of its existence, almost the whole literate world, and especially the novelist, accepts it as a force directing human behaviour as if it were as real as electricity. The very symbolism by which it is described seems to suggest electricity as a model: dynamic, powerful, dangerous, capable of some control but periodically asserting itself by violent outbreak. But other symbols too have been employed: the unconscious was submerged, nine-tenths below the surface, like an iceberg; it lurked in the impenetrable jungle from which it could emerge as a raging lion; it leered and lusted in diabolical, primitive sexual orgies, a heritage of our Darwinian past; it taunted, tempted, and tortured like an inquisitor. There was no escape; the id was indomitable, it was supreme; the ego was a willing though shuddering and quivering victim; the super-ego was a cringing and vacillating champion at best. And so the unconscious was groomed for the unwary, the credulous, and the crafty. Human beings behaved peculiarly, so a scapegoat or whipping boy had to be found; the "unconscious" was in the offing. Once it was brought into the open (a paradox indeed), one could behave as one wished; the unconscious was in operation, and any kind of behaviour could be excused, if not explained.

Such a beautiful concept! One could ascribe any characteristic, quality, or power to the action of the unconscious. Who could contradict? The boy did murder his parents; the husband was certainly unfaithful; the bank clerk embezzled; the sister was cruel; the brother was a coward. Such patterns are difficult to explain, more difficult to anticipate, and still more difficult to prevent. The unconscious as a subterranean force was a simple explanation. But there it ended. What to do? According to the hypothesis of the all-powerful unconscious, we are born with it and stuck with it.

What is the alternative to the unconscious? This book is written to suggest an alternative—the conscious.

An explanatory principle for human behaviour should be derived from a background of *observable data*. If the facts at hand are still meagre, let us say, "We don't know—yet." It is unnecessary to take refuge in the mystical. A framework can be constructed which, provided the base is sound and solid, may be altered from time to time to fit new discoveries. (Just like the incorporation of indoor plumbing in recently electrified rural communities.) But let each new addition be an understandable as well as useful idea. If later research proves that an older idea is untenable, throw it out.

Fortunately, there is a psychological phenomenon which has actually been at hand since the dawn of history—namely the *conscious*. One criticism of the concept "consciousness" is that it is so difficult to define. The answer to this difficulty is that it is not necessary to define what is immediately known. If you are conscious, that is it. If you are not, then definition is futile. If you can read these words, or even *see* them, you are conscious. This phenomenon is the most fabulous of all the universe may boast. The movement of the stars, the flow of the tides, the eruption of the mountains, the turbulence of the seas, and the nurturing power of the sun all fade and diminish when compared with the "consciousness" of human beings. This is the stuff that forms the psychologist's frame of reference.

We at least are sure of our own conscious state. We can guess with a good deal of assurance that other human beings are conscious. For the purpose of this discussion we may stop there. Let someone else defend the chimpanzees.

But lest there should be any doubt of the position of this thesis, let us say that the difference between the conscious states of man and animals is so great that one must be extremely cautious about interpreting one on the basis of the other. Ever since Darwin unwittingly set the stage for asserting that human emotions were essentially a matter of evolution, and Köhler came out of the mists of Teneriffe with a chimpanzee in one hand and a banana in the other, psychologists have been trying to interpret the intricate and complex conscious behaviour of man in terms of the relatively simple behaviour of animals. That some attempts have been good cannot be ignored. Pavlov's conditioned reflex experiments were epoch-making. How much this mechanism has to do with the acquisition of higher patterns of human experience is still a matter for a great deal of research. The laity has taken over the term and concept and now for them if it isn't an "unconscious" drive, it is a "conditioned" one.

But aside from such findings in collateral sciences, the secret of human behaviour will be found in the study of conscious behaviour. Chemistry and physics and biology and genetics all are sciences. Their contributions to the study of living—hence acting and feeling and thinking—human beings will be like those of handmaidens. We will not cure criminals through an intravenous injection or an oral dosage; we will not control nations by electronic manipulation, except through the effect it has on the conscious life of the individual person. Let us consider consciousness.

Consciousness—a term to conjure with! Surely when Bunyan wrote his immortal allegory he was using the images and ideas that were a part of his life's experience and not dragged up from an inherited jungle. Shakespeare was not in a trance when he wrote his plays. It is as easy to describe his motives through conscious states as to postulate a deep well of urgent unrecognized cravings. Cervantes wrote from the vantage point of the wide experience available to him, ready at hand for his craftsmanship to manipulate. When Harvey envisaged the circulation of the blood he was not day-dreaming under the influence of his unconscious. Abraham Lincoln thought long and anxiously before he wrote his proclamation of emancipation; he was not lurking in the byways of an unknown never-never land. It is not necessary to postulate an unconscious influence when the effects of consciousness are so obvious.

Consciousness is the stuff that we humans use to "get what we want." It is through consciousness that we learn to compose symphonies, to pray, to cure, to prevent, to build, to aspire, to love as only humans can, and to perform all of the antitheses of these. We are truly the captains of our souls because we need not be clods.

And what of this consciousness? What is it like? What does it do? How does it work? For centuries the answers to these questions have been sought. The seeming lack of ready answers stimulated the revival of the "unconscious" in modern guise. That the answers are still vague, ambiguous, and "unscientific" does not justify the questions' being thrown out as useless, futile, and unanswerable.

Here is a phenomenon at our mental doorstep. Each one of us has a psychological laboratory at his disposal. This does not mean that everyone can work effectively in this laboratory without training. If a naive person were suddenly placed in the midst of the most modern and up-to-date nuclear physics laboratory, could he carry on just because the plant was there? The examination of one's own consciousness is one of the most difficult feats of scientific methodology. It is also suspect because there is no adequate control but one's own integrity. Only by inference, by comparing them with those of other consciousnesses, may the mind's results, records, and conclusions be verified. This may be done only indirectly. How can you describe to another what "red" looks like? Both observers may "look at" the same object, but is what they "see" the same? Using the same language may help them to understand each other but they can never share the same immediate experience. This same difficulty is shared to some extent by all scientific investigation. All records and conclusions must pass through somebody's mind at some time, even though there are machines to do some of the manipulation. But as yet no one has invented a machine that "feels." When a machine is invented that will sigh in awe when standing in Chartres cathedral looking at the rose windows, and feel inside itself a glow of compassionate wonder—then of course we may begin to examine consciousness objectively. Some say that some day there will be machines that will reason. Perhaps! But not feel.

The manipulation of variables may always be imitated by mechanical means. But "thinking" is more than such a dreary rearrangement of items. There *are* limits to conscious activity, but as compared to the limits of a mechanical "brain," consciousness soars far above that landlocked apparatus. Consciousness is independent of machines, unless the sense organs, nerve cells, muscle bundles and all of the paraphernalia of a living organism are considered to be machines. The zest of immediately knowing is part of the joy of a spring day, a sunset, a thunderstorm, a kiss, and a smile.

Meanwhile we may train ourselves to use our own experiences to understand human conscious behaviour. By checking with others, by using whatever devices are available for testing our conclusions, we may arrive at a further knowledge of the phenomenon of *consciousness*.

Consciousness differs from every other aspect of the universe; it is difficult to describe it in terms of analogies taken from the physical world. Yet, it is only by means of analogies that it may be even partially understood. There are sufficient data available to try to describe with some accuracy and validity the basic nature of this esoteric yet commonplace phenomenon.

Locke thought of consciousness as a wax plate upon which experience writes; William James likened it to the effect of a marble moving under a carpet in a continuous flowing sinuous stream; more recently others suggested that consciousness is a mould for shaping jelly, a filing cabinet, a telephone exchange, a gramophone record, a tape-recorder.

Consciousness is immediately known. I see, I hear, I feel, I move, I wonder, I wish, I want; this is the stuff of consciousness. When the physicist looks at a thermometer which is a device for translating heat into a linear dimension which it surely does not possess of itself, he must make the interpretation as a conscious person. To be sure, a thermostat may control the heat, but some conscious person decides how hot or cold a room should be. No matter how many steps there are in a series of events, if it is to impinge on human beings it becomes transformed into conscious experience.

Since consciousness is considered as the significant and essential component of human experience (the be-all), some description and explanation is in order. In a book of this scope, the description will be condensed. If it is vague, this is owing only partly to condensation. Fundamentally it is the result of the difficulty of understanding consciousness and of the lack of word-symbols to describe it. To avoid inventing new words, a device which has been attempted but which has helped very little, I will use ordinary words. The reader may try to attach them to his own conscious experiences. If he cannot, then I have failed. At any rate, one can try.

Although it is difficult to examine consciousness, and much more difficult to communicate the results of such examination to someone else, one may describe it in many ways. Keeping in mind that you, the reader, are conscious (by deduction), you may test anything that follows in this chapter by an examination of your own consciousness.

Consciousness is usually defined as an *immediate awareness*—that is, awareness of the immediate surroundings through the sense organs such as the retina of the eye, the cochlea of the ear, and the taste buds. Each one of these sense organs mediates what is called a sense modality, or a group of sensations, for example *vision, audition, taste, smell, touch* (deep and light). These are the original five (excluding the mythical extra one for woman), but there are more than these. You may try to identify them: *balance*; *kinaesthesia* (movement of muscles); *tendon* sense; *temperature* senses, warm and cold (which are quite distinct and separate from each other and not just absence of one or the other); *pain*, the *organic* senses (hunger, thirst, bladder distension, anal-sphincter distension, sense of stimulation of the erogenous zones associated with sex experience, sense of suffocation). This array of sense information is continuously at hand, and but for a built-in sorting arrangement called "attention" it would be very confusing if not overpowering. Sometimes indeed we think that we are being overpowered. A child is born capable of distinguishing the sense group to which he is *attending* against the background of all the others. Attention is an amazingly efficient process and highly conscious. Starting with this ability a child, recognizing differences, can go on to recognize similarities and then to classify them. Such a filing system puts sensations into order and saves a lot of time.

However, many things are happening at one time in this conscious being. *If a child is to survive* (keep this phrase in mind for future reference), he must be provided with various things such as food, water, and oxygen. He is not only equipped with the proper apparatuses, such as organs and glands, to deal with these things, but he also has a conscious activity by which he can obtain them. This is called *striving*. Man may be called a striving being. As long as he is alive he will be seeking something every *moment* of his life.

In striving towards these provisions for survival an infant can select certain combinations of his senses. Later he will say "I want that," and in selecting some sense-combinations will find them pleasing. Those that he rejects he will label as unpleasant. Thus he will be conscious of two feelings, pleasantness and unpleasantness. The combination of sense data plus the feeling plus the striving will acquire a label, a word. It will come to be called an *object*.

We have advanced now from the consideration of the simple sense experience to the more complicated contribution which consciousness makes to living. Objects are differentiated as either pleasant or unpleasant, and are sought after or avoided. The pleasantness is part of the conscious counterpart of the wanting. One wants a thing, hence it is pleasant; one does not want it, and therefore it is unpleasant. Although the mechanism of wanting or discarding is an inherent part of consciousness, the objects that will be included in either category are placed there through living experience. One is not born wanting or not wanting corn flakes. This is an acquired want which may change. "There is no accounting for taste" is a false statement.

In time striving becomes more skilful. *Learning* has begun. Learning is another of the inherent components of consciousness. Without consciousness learning would not take place. A person learns to perceive in order to make use of all of his experience in satisfying his basic needs. The *use* he makes of these experiences is the main component of meaning. The meaning of a "thing" is the use to which it may be put in order to reach a goal. The goal now becomes more important than the need. The infant's wants increase in proportion to his learning capacity and opportunity. A newborn infant is hungry, *needs* food, but soon learns to *want* certain food objects which he will later say he "likes"; others he "dislikes." By classifying objects he chooses which one to work towards. He is now able to envisage a goal. He may want a rattle, a bottle, a kiddy-car, a soft spot to lie on, a companion, a bicycle, a dime, a new coat, a mate, a house, a vice-presidency . . . Hunger is one of the needs. Filet mignon becomes a want.

Now we have to retrace our steps again. The description of consciousness has become rather complicated; sensations, needs, wants, striving, feelings, attending, choosing, all at the same time. However, there is more to come.

What does consciousness look like? Actually there are moments of consciousness which follow each other relatively slowly. Consciousness jerks, somewhat as a movie film jerks passing through a projector. Just as each picture in the film strip is covered over when it moves to be replaced by the next one, which in turn is stationary for a moment and then moves on, so the moments of consciousness succeed each other. Whatever is in the centre of attention at this moment fades out in the next, to be replaced by another content. One must be wary of such analogies, so do not take this comparison too literally.

But the modern movie film appears as if it were not interrupted at regular intervals by a barrier that is interposed between the film and the screen. For an appreciable moment the image on the screen is stationary. As a child you no doubt made your own movie. You placed two dots on the margin of a page in a book and on each succeeding page placed the dots slightly further apart. Then flipping the pages you "perceived" the dots moving away from each other. You may have illustrated a figure of a man kicking a football towards the top of the page. You perceived motion. You may say "I saw the ball move." But the ball and man did not move. They altered position but at all times were stationary. Such an experience may be called an illusion. We conclude that perception may not always be "accurate." Sometimes motion is illusory. However moments of consciousness occupy time, they succeed each other like this: – – – – – – . There is a limiting membrane separating one moment from another. It is this membrane which aids one's perception of the passing of time. There is always conscious anticipation of the next moment, and conscious memory of the one before. Consciousness is always made up of three moments, the one that has just gone, the immediate one, and the one that is anticipated. Learning, education, and measures of intelligence depend on these.

And so with consciousness, the "moments" succeed each other inevitably and irresistibly. Very soon—none of us can remember when —we learned to interpret this series of events as *one continuous stream*. A moment of consciousness lasts for a fraction of a second. Overcoming the jerkiness of consciousness may have important bearing on later maturation. Perhaps this jerkiness of moments is involved in stuttering or latent development, such as reading-readiness.

The form of consciousness is such that at all times it is "occupied." There is a content which "fills" the conscious moment. From the beginning this content is divided into two distinct parts, one to which the individual gives precedence (selects) for interpreting, while the other forms the background or context from which the former is derived. The succession of conscious events is inevitably interpreted as a *temporal* sequence. Thus time enters into consciousness because of the form of consciousness. Whatever "time" may be, human consciousness cannot escape its impact. No matter what may be the content of a conscious moment, it seems to be placed—pinpointed in time —and it also appears to be fixed in space.

How accurate the senses are in recording the impact of the environment is open to question (for example, colour-blind persons do not "see" the same world as others do); the interpretation of these sense data is notoriously inaccurate. This is not to be wondered at, since one interprets always in terms of the "want" of the moment, and as each one of us may want a different goal, in a similar environment we envisage the environment differently. Illusions are the rule rather than the exception. This, of course is the basis of the recurring question, What *is* the world about us? Is there a *real* world? Or is reality only our interpretation? Is reality a concept invented by the psychiatrist comparable to the old concept of matter of the physicist? He now tells us that there is no matter, only energy. Whatever the philosophical answer, a person perceives the world as he does and he believes in its reality. And for all practical purposes that is enough for him to act upon, in order to get what he wants.

There is another aspect of the form of consciousness—the future. Keeping in mind that one moment follows upon another in inevitable sequence, it is obvious even after a cursory observation of your own consciousness that you are anticipating your on-coming experience. You are projecting into the future. In a real sense you are fortune-telling. At this moment you can anticipate what you will do after you put this book down—go to sleep, go for a walk, have a meal or a snack, etc. You will at times think of your next holiday plan, the house you will buy, the stock you will sell, the lecture you will give, the boy or girl you will meet, what you will spend or save. In each case you will be projecting your immediate awareness into the future. Although you can only live in the present because of the elasticity of consciousness, it can in all seriousness be suggested that you live in the future. The present is so evanescent, and the past is gone.

We can at times and under propitious circumstances dredge up experiences from the past. But they are reinstated in the present and projected usually on the screen of tomorrow. Nostalgia is the wistful interpretation of a twice-told tale.

We know that the changes that occur in the surrounding world as well as those continually taking place in his body have an impact on a person's consciousness. There are, of course, many changes which do not affect consciousness at all, such as those beyond the perceptual limits of vision and hearing, and those that result from the functioning of the involuntary nervous system—for example the change in size of the pupil of the eye, the passing of an impulse along the nerve, or the contraction of blood vessels. The exact effect of this impact, of these changes of which we are not directly aware, is still a matter of conjecture. Although such changes vary in apparent quantitative effect, there seems to be no relation between the energy employed in the change and the intensity of the conscious experience; for example a clap of thunder may pass almost unnoticed whereas the thin scratching of a mouse in a strange room at night may dominate one's consciousness.

There appears to be some more or less permanent trace of the impact on one's senses, because the initial impact may be reinstated, or recalled, more or less faithfully. However, most of the traces cannot be recalled; they are forgotten, and that is a very good thing. It prevents cluttering. Forgetting is not a passive but rather a highly selective process. The "intensity" of the initial impact is not the most important factor in recalling.

We can all recognize various "areas" of consciousness. First those from which an experience can be readily and immediately recalled under ordinary circumstances, for example one's name, a recent interesting experience, or important items in a professional situation. Then there is an area from which recall is more difficult, and finally an area which is not subject to recall except under exceptional circumstances. As well as areas, there are also various "states" of consciousness, such as those that prevail while a person is asleep, under drugs or anaesthetic, or under hypnotism; or those that result after serious damage to the nervous system, shock, or fainting. It is well to remember that in all of these states one does not *lose* consciousness; consciousness is lost only at death—if then. One is conscious while asleep, but in a dream state. Since consciousness is a continuous process as long as one is alive, one dreams every night, all night. That one cannot recall the content of one's dream is not to be wondered at. One forgets the trivia of everyday experience; for example, what were you thinking of at 8:45 this morning? Unless there was some kind of crisis, you will find it rather difficult to recall the content of your consciousness at that time. Most dreams are trivial. The significance of dreams in the understanding of human behaviour has been much exaggerated, especially by charlatans.

The ability to distinguish small differences in sensory experiences, classify them, interpret them, pigeonhole them, and recall them when necessary for achieving a goal is the basis of intelligent behaviour. The whole process has no mechanical artificial counterpart except very superficially.

The most important aspect of consciousness is that it is the basis for the reaction of the individual to his environment. Although a good deal of the activity of the response apparatus (muscles and glands) does not impinge on consciousness, the portion which does so is most significant, first because it is so important to the individual's economy, that is to his learning, and secondly because it may be observed by another person, recorded, measured, manipulated, and to some extent controlled. It is this observable outcome that has become the limited but recordable subject-matter of most scientific psychology.

The consciousness of movement is called kinaesthesia. One may still learn without the use of other sense modalities; for example blind and deaf people can learn quite readily. A person could not learn if he had no sense of his own muscle action. A person is never wholly quiescent. There are always some muscles moving, and in this background of the consciousness muscle sense contributes a great deal to the concept of *self*.

As yet no one has ever examined a child's consciousness directly, any more than anyone has examined that of another adult. We may, however, assume that, at least at birth or possibly even before, the transitory and sequential character of conscious moments holds true for the infant. There is every reason to believe this to be so. A child's consciousness is not a booming, buzzing confusion or a whirling, nebular spinning wheel, it is rather a narrow, bare, repetitive series of simple sensory experiences such as seeing, hearing, smelling, and touching. There is little interpretation of these sensations and thus their meaning is vague. There cannot be a "buzzing" for a child because at this time he will not know what a buzzing a continuous experience is! Perhaps his consciousness is jerky as were the early moving pictures. We can let our imagination run riot because we will never know. An adult is not able to recall his own infantile consciousness and the infant can't tell us what his is like. In the pseudo-scientific press statements are made occasionally by individuals who claim that they can recall their own passage through the birth canal. As the Duke of Wellington said, "If you believe that, you will believe anything." Obviously he was referring to another matter.

We have already learned that a child interprets immediate sense experiences as objects, such as an apple or a block. To this he adds other experiences; thus he learns how to use these objects to gratify his wants. At the same time he finds that he can "see" the apple even though it is not there, that is, present in sensory experience. This is an image and is the result of a vivid recall of a past experience. A child must be confused by this fascinating but at times alarming experience. By the same process he finds no difficulty in believing in "things" we tell him about, such as fairies, witches, and Santa Claus. Often he has companions which are not there, but he acts as if they were; he acquires an imaginary companion.

Through images and the recall of experiences in the form of symbols or meanings a child learns to manipulate the world even though the immediate surroundings do not correspond to the central content of his consciousness at the time. Apparently he may be wholly oblivious to the immediate. Sitting in class, he may be far away fishing. He may even learn to control his expression so as to deceive the teacher into believing that he is concentrating on the lesson. Husbands and wives still find this technique rewarding.

Through this ability to manipulate his past experiences, a child learns to imagine, invent, reason, create without limit. He is only limited when he attempts to involve the external world in his strivings; no matter how much he tries he cannot get out physically from three-dimensional space or on-going time. Even though, like the poet, he may give the command, "Backward, turn backward, O time in your flight," time does not obey. Some dramatists have portrayed what might happen if it did.

When a child has learned to recall images, feelings, patterns of acting, he can divorce himself from the physical world to a large extent. He can think up problems and solve them without their actual presence to sense. He is not limited by having to be there. He can literally build castles in the air; he can cross rivers, shoot animals, compose music, or make up stories. His scope of classification extends widely. Whereas earlier he classified objects as "pleasant" and "unpleasant," as "I want" and "I don't want," now an apple, a pear, a peach are classed as fruit, a word which of course has no *sense* counterpart. Thus a group of percepts have grown into a *concept*. Concepts are useful because they are a shorthand method of classification. Later on he will combine simple concepts into even more abstract groupings such as justice, liberty, morality. It is well to remember that these lofty concepts all begin as simple sense experience. Thus concepts, however commonly they are held, are highly personal, and may differ widely among individuals. Each concept is given a name, such as justice, and it is then mistakenly assumed that justice means the same

CHART I

QUESTIONS CONSCIOUSNESS DICTATES

---

(1) WHICH?   Perception of *differences*: this ability is given. In the first form consciousness takes, the individual can see the difference between A and *not A*.

(2) WHEN?   Perception of *time*: this percept emerges because it is inevitable that moments of consciousness succeed each other, from the moment they begin to the end.

(3) WHERE?   Perception of *space*: three-dimensional perceptual space is given. There is a much longer developmental sequence here than with (2), therefore time is more fundamental than space.

(4) WHAT?   Perception of *object*: this depends on (1).

(5) WHO?   Perception of *person*: this specialization occurs at two years. It later includes the question, WHOSE?

(6) HOW?   Perception of *process*: this involves a notion of causality and depends on (2).

(7) WHY?   Perception of *purpose*: this last perception develops much later than the others.

Whether questions one to six are asked by lower organisms, we do not know; we do know that question seven is asked only by humans and is the origin of all forms of religion and philosophy. Questions one to seven appear in developmental order. Verification of that order is an enormous challenge to research. We would need pre-language devices to study it.

The individual selects from his experience the answers to these questions that suit him best. The phenomenon of *selection* is the most significant aspect of security theory, since selection is the basis for making decisions.

---

to everybody, whereas each person has his own "concept" of justice which may or may not be the same as his neighbour's.

Because the human being is conscious he asks questions about himself and his environment. These questions arise in a time sequence with his increasing age, as is shown in Chart I. He asks the questions, Which? When? Where? What? Who? How? and Why? in that order. He answers these by selecting from his experience whatever suits him best. This phenomenon of selection is the most significant aspect of the security theory, for selection means making decisions.

3 · Consequences

In which the difference between needs and wants is investigated, and a search is made for an overriding goal; in which the nature of consequences is found to include sequentiality, use as future references, predictability, causality, and acceptance and rejection; in which a definition is given of security and its conscious correlate, serenity.

THE BASIC NEEDS of man are: (1) to select, through accepting or rejecting immediate conscious experiences, (2) to satisfy the organic appetites, and (3) to deal with frustration. Man will continuously seek to satisfy these three needs. At all times one or more of them are operative; at some times some are more imperative than others; hungry, a man seeks food; in pain, he seeks surcease; tired, he seeks rest; under the urgency of the sex need he seeks a mate; frustrated, he attacks or tries to escape. From the beginning he not only seeks to satisfy the need of which he is conscious, however vaguely, but he learns to strive towards a particular answer to it. When hungry he needs food but he wants warm milk, an apple, an ice cream cone, a steak, and even a soufflé; when tired he wants a comfortable place to rest: warm, soft, dark, quiet; when in pain he seeks a sedative, an anaesthetic, a "cure"; when seeking sex satisfaction he wants a certain object, an only-one-in-the-world woman, not anyone—or perhaps it may be another male, or a furry object; and he seeks certain emotional symbols such as flags or skin colour which satisfy anger, or others which arouse fears and phobias. These specific goals are *wants*.

A commonly held belief magnifies the significance of the needs as urgent driving forces. *The wants are far more imperative.* A child will starve himself for some vague want; this is a forerunner of an adult's threat of voluntary starvation (as in a hunger strike) unless a want is granted. A saint denies all of his needs in order to satisfy the want of salvation through martyrdom; so will a soldier in battle for a principle. Derived wants, such as ambition, status, achievement, later prove more powerful than a loaf of bread. These will be more fully discussed later on in this book.

Man, then, is a striving animal, continuously seeking a *goal*. Up to this point we have been discussing needs and their corresponding wants, which are fragmented or transitory, even though recurring. Taken all together, they do not adequately describe total human behaviour. There must be an overriding goal that consolidates human endeavour and gives it coherent meaning.

The object of this book is to describe such a goal and to search for its origins. An overriding goal, should have definite characteristics:

1. The most important is that it should be at all times conscious; not necessarily in the centre of consciousness, but always capable of being brought there.

2. It should give positive direction to man's striving. Life provides the energy, and the goal determines the direction in which it will be used.

3. It should have objective and hence observable aspects so that it may be described, recorded, and studied.

4. It should have universal application. All mankind (as well as infrahuman species) should be governed by this goal.

5. It should cover all human activity both inner and outer, normal and "abnormal." Abnormal behaviour is not the result of a different kind of goal but rather of unusual methods of achieving the same goals.

6. At its best it should provide the illusion of freedom.

Fortunately there is a phenomenon which describes such an overriding goal, with these six characteristics. This is the sequential nature of moments of consciousness.

One moment of consciousness following upon another in an inevitable sequence, as we mentioned, permitted the perception of time. Time perception enables us to be aware of the past, present, and future. Whatever were the earliest meanings of these moments, very soon they—the past, the present, and the future—were differentiated, and the most significant of them became the future. The expectation and anticipation of the next moment, and then the next moments, frames the outstanding experiences of *time*. This projection into the future provided a background for early enlargement of perception, a broadening of experience, the basis of learning.

The ability to anticipate more accurately what is to come to pass appears early in life. Predicting may be recognized when a child cries when he wants food. Later he uses this device for gratifying other wants. A child initiating certain arm and hand movements is anticipating that they will result in his grasping a toy. Reaching is far more complicated than crying and of course appears later in a child's repertoire of abilities.

The accuracy of prediction depends on a number of factors, including a child's initial endowment. The perception of the relationship of the following event—that is, the consequence—to the antecedent event, takes a set course. Partly through maturation, a child projects his consciousness further and further into the future. From the observation of two moments in consciousness that follow each other immediately, learning proceeds to the perception of "soon and late," "after breakfast," "before a bath," "tonight," "tomorrow," "the weekend," "the summer holidays," "finishing school," and so on, to the ultimate perception, infinity. The succeeding stages vary in the length of time required for the learning. Some people never reach the final steps.

Certain events seem to have an inevitable sequence. Night follows day follows night; water seems always to "wet" one, whether as rain or in a bath or from emptying the bladder; food seems to satisfy hunger; and so on. But there are some antecedent events which are not always followed by the same consequent. Sometimes crying does not succeed in gratifying a want; one does not always grasp the toy for which one reaches; one step does not always follow upon another; thunder does not always follow lightning. The sun does not always shine. So a child must include inevitability and inconsistency into his concept of the universe. This confusion, which is vaguely but unavoidably perceived by the infant, child, and youth, and by many adults, provides a basis for the most enduring of controversies: What is the nature of the universe? One outcome of the unresolved controversy is that a great many people want to establish the reality of inevitability in their own minds. They want to be assured, as will be discussed later on.

A child is readily assured by an "explanation" given to him by someone in whom he has faith. Later on he will examine this "explanation" in the light of his own experience. The scientist "explains" the apparent inconsistency of the phenomena in the changing universe as due to the current lack of detailed knowledge. Given time, he will "prove" their consistency. He will deny what is obvious to any child, namely that one event in time "causes" the following consequent—that lightning causes thunder, that fumbling a dish causes it to fall and break, that eating green apples causes a belly-ache—and he will likewise deny such adult concepts of causality as that scarcity causes inflation, that poverty causes ennui, or that liquor causes drunkenness.

Whether or not it is inevitable that man should introduce "causality" as an explanatory principle into his thinking and interpreting of the universe with himself in it, the fact remains that he does so. Immediately, he is presented with the dilemma of having to postulate a causal agent. This leads to another question in interpreting consequences: What is the nature of this agent?

Whatever one's answers are to the above questions, the fact is that a child grows up evaluating the consequence of his actions. Whatever his interpretation of the workings of the universe, he is learning that there are some predictions which are accurate and others which are more vicarious, facetious, or temperamental. But he also learns that whether he is accurate or not in his predictions, *some* consequence will occur.

In the course of time he will also learn that some consequences fit into his aim of reaching goals, and that some will deter his goals or prevent them from being achieved. He will classify these consequences as desirable (pleasant), and undesirable (unpleasant). Obviously he will try to arrange for the occurrence of the desirable and the eradication of the undesirable. He finds that through his own efforts he cannot disturb the flow of antecedent and consequent in the universe. Only Joshua made the sun stand still! But he finds that if he is willing to accept the consequences of re-arranging the antecedents, he may ultimately experience a consequence even more desirable, or at least avoid a consequence which is undesirable. For example: it is raining; he wishes to go outside, but he does not wish to get wet (an older child, obviously), so he "decides" to stay in—he thus avoids a consequence which he anticipated as undesirable. Or a young man wishes to play golf well; in consequence he must spend many hours practising, this occupies time in which he might be "enjoying himself"; he is thus willing to accept this consequence (self-denial) in order to achieve a persistently present goal—a desirable consequence of his self-discipline. In this fashion a child will learn that consequences, no matter what they may turn out to be, must be accepted and made the best of. Self denial to gain a future goal is the antithesis of the present-day orgy of credit-buying: "travel now, pay later," "nothing down, no payments till February" (or as the English so quaintly say, "hire-purchase").

It will be pointed out below how much help a child must have to learn to accept consequences, and also how the assistance, essential to a child's physical, mental, and social survival should be administered.

Because—the use of this word shows that empirically we subscribe to the causal nature of the universe!—because antecedents may be manipulated, a child soon learns that there are many ways in which some undesirable consequences may be partially avoided. For example if he wants an object, he may take it and hide it and deny taking it; if he fails in a task, he may blame someone else; or in order to avoid an unpleasant task, he may feign illness. (These devices will be fully discussed below.) Thus we grow up and classify the consequences of our actions into two categories, those which we will accept, come what may, and those which we will attempt to avoid at whatever cost.

We are now ready for the thesis of this book:

1. *When a person is willing to accept the consequences of his actions (decisions) without equivocation he is said to be* secure. *The conscious state accompanying this pattern is* serenity.

2. *Obversely—when a person tries to avoid the consequences of his actions (decisions) he is* insecure. *He is then no longer serene, but* anxious.

Now we are also in a position to define mental health in a positive fashion. A person is mentally healthy when he is secure. An insecure person is in a state of mental *ill* health. The degree of his disability is determined by the amount, intensity, and rigidity of his avoidance reactions.

Let us examine the characteristics of this thesis in the light of those suggested earlier as essential to a satisfactory overriding goal.

1. Serenity and anxiety are definitely conscious experiences.

2. The positive goal is the accepting of consequences.

3. It is relatively easy for an observer, and certainly the person involved, to identify acceptance and avoidance reactions, as well as to recognize serene and anxious states.

4. All living organisms are placed in the position of accepting or rejecting consequences.

5. The inevitable nature of consequences and the acceptance or rejection thereof provides ample room for "explaining" behaviour without invoking a pathological factor to include "abnormals."

6. The individual has freedom of choice within limits of action.

The security theory which will be outlined in the following chapters has proven itself adequate to deal with problems in child training, and it has suggested fruitful methods for dealing with clinical problems of both adults and children. A diagrammatic scheme of the theory is given in Chart II on page 34. It should be referred to as the text is read.

CHART II

The Security Scheme

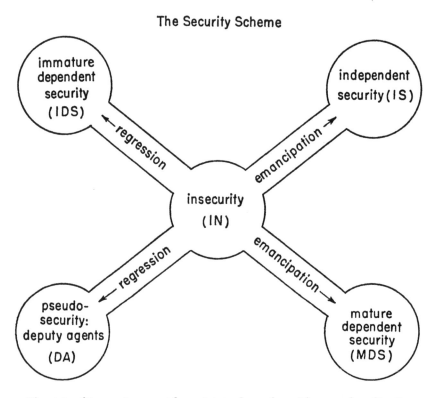

The state of insecurity cannot be maintained very long. There are four directions in which one can move from insecurity to a state of security:

1. Towards IMMATURE DEPENDENT SECURITY (IDS). This direction is desirable in the infant, but a sign of regression in the adult. It consists of letting an agent make one's decisions and accept the consequences.

2. Towards INDEPENDENT SECURITY (IS). This consists of making decisions and accepting the consequences one's self. It depends on effort towards a goal.

3. Towards MATURE DEPENDENT SECURITY (MDS). In this state two or more people make reciprocal decisions and share the consequences.

4. Towards PSEUDO-SECURITY or the use of DEPUTY AGENTS (DA). This avoids a direct attack on the problem by using a means of arriving at an apparent but temporary solution.

The processes by which one moves from insecurity to a state of security are thus *emancipation* and *regression*. Emancipation is the forward movement to independent or mature dependent security; regression is the backward movement to a former state of immature dependent security, or to a form of deputy agent employed at an earlier time.

4 · Immature Dependent Security

In which an attempt is made to describe the security status of a newborn infant, and furthermore, to follow the early development of security through his dependence upon an agent (usually the mother); in which the importance of consistent treatment for the development of early security is stressed.

TRY TO ENVISAGE the mind of a young infant. We can only guess what it is like. Our guess must be based on what we know of our own adult conscious state. We are not looking for something that is unobservable, but for something that up to the present has been unrecorded. Whether it is unrecordable is still a matter of controversy. We believe that the child whom we are observing is aware of his own mental activities— that is, he is conscious.

There is good reason to believe that the infant in the last months of intra-uterine life is conscious, since infants who are born prematurely appear to be as conscious as those born at full term. In fact there is no reason why we should not ascribe consciousness to the embryo or, for that matter, to the egg, fertilized by a conscious sperm. But this discussion, however interesting, would lead us far astray. At what stage of pre-natal development consciousness begins is not known. We can, however, ascribe consciousness to the foetus at least some time prior to actual birth.

We may infer that if the foetus *in utero* is conscious, he is secure and feels serene because all his needs are satisfied and most of his sensory experiences are constant except for mild organic changes. As consistency later becomes important for the child's learning, so consistency in the mother's mood and attitude during pregnancy is important to his pre-natal security. Although he is not fully aware of it, he is experiencing the consequences of his limited choices. There are at times convulsive movements that indicate some reaction to a confining environment. Whether these are merely reflex, or whether they are voluntary decisive actions, need not concern us. In either case, they fit into a pattern of learning that becomes more obvious after birth. The unborn child's state of mind would undoubtedly be serene, since the consequences of his choices, though exceedingly limited in variety, would be stable and hence from moment to moment predictable. Also he would find the consequences mostly acceptable. Because he is conscious he would have some feelings, and these would be pleasant since his needs would be satisfied and his limited wants gratified.

However, towards the end of uterine life decided changes take place. The onset of the uterine contractions must be relatively unpleasant to the unborn child, and then the expulsion through the birth canal, because of its novel aspects and often sudden onset, must arouse in the child at first an experience of fear. The gulping for breath, the first inspiration of air, the vocalizing, the change in his touch and kinaesthesia, the temperature and sound sense-fields provide such a change that his conscious experience must suddenly become confusing. Never again during life can there be such a cataclysmic change of total sensory stimulation. Serenity is shattered. And for a short period there is insecurity with its accompanying profound anxiety. Fortunately memory is short, and soon the soothing hands, the warm swaddling clothes and the comfortable support of bed or basket in a large measure help to blot out the indignity of birth and its accompanying relative rough handling.

And now other portentous changes take place. A newborn child who has lived in a tightly curtailed environment now finds that the boundary of his world suddenly becomes infinite. He appreciates at this time only the change. There is also a difference in time schedule. Before birth his needs have been looked after continuously; now there are interrupted periods during which a need may remain unanswered. His waking movements are so different. When he falls asleep he may again take up a semblance of the flexor uterine posture, resume his uterine dreams, to be awakened by a new or at least a more urgent experience—hunger or thirst. The physiological appetites begin to direct the life of this organic morsel in earnest. His needs must be met. But how? On the one hand his pre-natal physiological arrangements no longer serve. On the other, he is completely incapable of taking care of them himself. Therefore, there must be an *agent*—an outside mediator between his needs and their satisfaction. This agent must be a living person, and most frequently it is the person with whom he has been pre-natally most closely associated: his mother.

Two confluent streams of influence are now brought to bear on his development: the impact of the external world, and his consequent seeking for wider gratifications of his wants. Since in these early weeks his ability to project into the future is an anticipation only from one moment to the next, he can withstand changes that would later on be quite portentous. He is protected from too sudden or too overpowering an impact by his very immaturity. His restricted memory protects him from experiences which later on would be shattering unless he were adequately prepared to take them in his stride. In England during the bombing of World War II, infants in arms were only mildly concerned with the noise of bombs and two-year-olds were stimulated by the "fireworks"—provided they were safely held or tightly enclosed by their mothers or by others equally familiar to them.

In order to survive in the outside world, the infant must be provided with an agent to continue the services rendered *in utero*. But he must provide his own cushion to soften the impact of the accumulation of an infinite variety of external stimuli. Both the agent and his own cushioning are important; the former to some extent guarantees his physical survival, the latter establishes his mental state during this period of survival. Both are operating at birth.

An infant acquires confidence in his physical environment relatively early, because the antecedents and consequences are essentially consistent. At times he may think he has been betrayed because his judgment has been at fault, especially when he misjudges distances. Although at first he may ascribe his inadequacy to the vagaries of the universe, rather than to his own ignorance, later on he revises his estimates in favour of an ordered universe.

But his relationship with his human agent is more precarious, because consistency of interaction is so difficult. The saving grace is that in this relationship the "warmth" of the feeling can often compensate for occasional lapses in consistency. The "warm feeling" is a complicated experience which grows from the effect of simple contiguity; that is, the agent becomes familiar and hence a refuge in a world of growing confusion. To this is added in due course the more constant elements of belonging, tenderness, affection, and trust. From this familiarity and warmth a child learns to *depend* upon the agent. The efficacy of the dependence rests upon the behaviour and personality of the agent. Only when he is "betrayed" will a child be alarmed and his feeling of faith and trust in the agent be upset. The warmth may be defined as the atmosphere that pervades the family group. It is an intangible part of a child's life but is far more significant than the furniture, the automobile, or the front door in establishing the extent of a child's security.

As he interprets the world about him, an infant learns to trust his judgments in accordance with his setbacks and triumphs. He looks forward to those choices which are associated with the "satisfactions" of an earthy kind: food, comfort, safety, and close contact. Each time such a service is rendered, something pleasant happens; but there may be rather unpleasant accompaniments, such as an irritating restriction of activity (while being dressed) or unpleasant tickling about the face (while being washed) and a postponement of the pleasantness of the satisfaction of hunger. But in a short time all his disappointments will be smoothed away and he will be coolish-warm, loosely but comfortably held, feeding luxuriously, and surrounded by a nice, familiar smell and feeling of "home." He learns that *he can count on it.* In a relatively short while, he finds that this kind of predictable series of events occurs more and more frequently.

He will have begun to refine his judgments. He will separate his world of experiences into many categories, but two contrasting groups will for a time dominate the field. One group will include experiences that are readily anticipated, such as light following dark, followed by light and then dark in interminable sequence; the ceiling paper design; the side of his crib; the feel of his bed—these will form a constant background. The other group will include interrupted experiences, objects present and then absent, sometimes more or less regularly interrupted than at other times with quite unexpectedly long or short intervals between appearances. Thus he may separate the world into the two categories, the living and the inanimate. The labels of course will be attached much later.

One particular group of the "living" experiences are centred on one object which becomes the most familiar of all—the agent, the *deus ex machina*—his mother.

Having examined and catalogued the sights, sounds, smells, and other sensory experiences of his restricted world, he will begin to feel bored, but he will discover that this agent is a never-empty coffer of good things, who will supply the antidote to boredom by changing the world about him, by carrying him to and fro, by providing a change in the sound world through singing or crooning. The crooner finds that the same tune, or the same few bars are far more appreciated than long preludes or varied programmes, and she learns that although she may introduce a few variations, at intervals, they must not be *too* varied. Later on the same bed-time story is expected and even demanded. The child wants the feeling of familiarity, flavoured only with a touch of novelty. More of the theme, and only a little of the variations. At times he may be able to take more of the new, but a road back to the familiar must always be open.

Held in his mother's arms, he feels that he may explore and seek adventure, but suddenly he seems to have reached a limit, his laugh dries up, he cuddles closer and buries his face in his mother's breast, and the game is over. This accepting of the new, the potentially fearful, is exciting, but there must be a familiar, trusted world from which he can foray, and to which he can always return. The dependable agent is a *must* if early security is to be established.

This agent may be the mother, or it may be the foster-mother, nurse, attendant, nanny, or whoever looks after a child. The role of the agent is to accept the consequences for the child's acts, and to make some of the decisions that he will later learn to make for himself. But from the beginning, some of the decisions are his. He can choose to cry or keep quiet, to sleep or stay awake. His own decisions are relatively few at first, but these few are important for the beginning of a pattern of decision-making, and a great deal that happens later depends on these early attempts.

The role of the parental agent is far more significant than that of just keeping the child alive. During the first years the agent must supply a "jumping-off platform." The trust the child learns to place in his early agent remains throughout life as the prototype of the confidence he will place later on in other agents and ultimately in himself. And, by the same token, a lack of opportunity to develop such trust will be reflected in his later contacts with others.

Hence the necessity of early schedules. All of life's new facets, all its colours, tones, notes, movement, faces, dark and shadows, lights and shades, minor rumblings and agitations; its movements to and fro, up and down, bang and quiet, rough and smooth, cold and warm and clammy wet; all these are exciting, but beneath them there must be things reliable enough for him to count on, such as being held securely in a tight embrace and at times gently rocked to and fro; the warm smell of a guzzling intimacy; the relaxing luxury of being gradually lowered into the familiar medium of the bath, and afterwards the glowing feeling of a stimulated skin surface. Slowly he learns to count on these gratifying states. He may become impatient waiting for them and sometimes utter triumphant cries of outraged disregard, but he always knows that *inevitably* the "good" will come to pass.

And so in such first months a child is secure most of the time, and feels serene; it is a serenity which passes all understanding. This form of security is called *immature dependent security*. It is *immature* because it implies a naive acceptance of a service which is rendered without request and without direct recompense, a service of which a child is unaware, and which he only fully recognizes when in the course of time he (or particularly she) renders it himself. Obviously, having such a solicitous agent is a very satisfactory state. All of his demands are being met. The consequences of his actions, if not pleasing, may be sloughed off with impunity. No wonder most children find the story of the magic lamp so easy to believe and cherish. Where ignorance is bliss indeed!

At this point we will digress for a moment to recall that a child is continuously classifying, interpreting, and reinterpreting his experiences. In order that he may develop "trust," there must be a certain stability or sameness in the consequences of some of his experiences with his agents, particularly with the parental agents, and *more* particularly with his mother. Thus in her treatment of her young child, she must be consistent. Some of my colleagues have intimated that consistency is one of the most difficult of human traits to manifest. All too true! But that should not prevent one from being as consistent as possible. One must make allowance for the vagaries of a child's behaviour, keeping in mind that they may be due to the defects in consistency of the parent. There is no necessity to introduce arbitrary inconsistencies to prepare a child for the "outer" world. The tendency for humans to err will take care of this contingency.

The importance of the parent-child relationship cannot be over-emphasized. Unfortunately this relationship, often dismissed with a word or phrase implying simplicity, is extremely complex. The disturbance of the relationship is often considered the only cause of later serious trouble. For example, delinquency is often attributed to a child being "unwanted," or spoiled and over-indulged. "The parents were too strict—or too lenient"; "The parents never practised what they preached"; and so on. These diagnoses are as false as all half-truths—or quarter-truths.

It is well to recognize that all human relationships are still jungles untracked by the psychologist. We do not know our way through the jungle of this early relationship at present, but let us in any case see how we can classify it. At least we can show that it is not a flat and unobstructed meadow.

If it is most important for the young child to feel secure in his early immature dependency, the agent should behave so as to foster this security and its accompanying state of serenity. Early security is essential to the later emancipation process which the agent must coincidentally supervise and foster. The agent's job may be compared to the job of guiding two horses going in opposite directions. Strangely enough it *is* important to stay in the same place. Difficult, yes. Impossible? No!

The agent must not lose sight of the importance of learning, for the security patterns are in the main learned. A child learns to trust and have confidence in an agent, and so it is essential that the outstanding characteristic of an agent be *consistency*. This cannot be over-emphasized. However, it is easier to state this condition than to describe it, and it is far more difficult to lay down a precise method of administration, because it concerns all of the facets of parental influence, both witting and unwitting.

Chart III illustrates an attempt to analyse the intricacies of the parental attitudes and antics as seen and felt by a child. In the first column are seven departments or fields of influence. There may be others, and they undoubtedly overlap. Opposite each field there is assumed to be a scale stretching between two opposites and passing through a mid-point. The two opposites are undesirable, the mid-points represent the desirable or wholesome pattern.

For example, the first category, administration, includes the obvious disciplinary procedures. These range from the retaliatory punishments of the most extreme kind to the absence of all consequences, passing through the mid-point which is an arrangement of reasonable, relevant, and productive consequences made by a rational parent. And so through the six categories, which are self-explanatory.

In each area there are two ways by which the parent contributes to the child's development: the witting influences which the parents hope will bear fruit, and which include the overt rules and regulations, the precepts, exhortations, homilies, lectures, and moralities; and the unwitting influence, namely the example which the parents show. Of the two, the second appears to be more important.

We must now try to envisage the effect of these seven aspects of parental contribution to the security of the child. Keeping in mind that the child is learning to use parents as agents, it is obvious that the more consistent the influence, the more effective it will be. If in

CHART III

PARENTAL FIELDS OF INFLUENCE AFFECTING THE CHILD'S SECURITY

FIELDS OF INFLUENCE	DESIRABLE		
	←——————— MID-POINT ———————→		
1. Administration of discipline	Cruel Tyrannical Ruthless Vengeful	Patient Impersonal Non-violent	Indulgent Lenient
2. Feeling	Indifferent	Affectionate *Tender	Demonstrative Overwhelming
3. Bestowal of status	Hostile	*Accepting	Possessive
4. Organization of family	Contentious Spiteful Jealous	Considerate Tolerant	Unorganized Chaotic
5. Loyalties	Fearful Hateful	Comforting	Treacherous
6. Emotions	Volatile	Enthusiastic	Restrained Apathetic
7. Protection	Neglectful	Solvent Concerned	Restrictive

*From a clinical point of view the two most significant of the mid-point influences are *giving a child a feeling of belonging* and *expressing tenderness*. This latter can never be insincere.

the classroom the teacher should one day announce that $2 + 2 = 4$, and the next day that $2 + 2 = 5$, indiscriminately and inconsistently, the learner would be baffled and the resultant learned pattern confused. The more consistent the teaching, the more readily and effectively does the pupil learn. But there is no reason to suppose that one *kind* of behaviour is more readily learned than another. Providing that there is consistency, a cruel parent can be trusted to be cruel as readily as a consistently kind parent to be kind. It is the consistency that builds security. However, the *kind* of behaviour will determine in each child the resultant total security pattern. A child consistently rejected by one or both parents must inevitably find a substitute. If there are vicarious and unpredictable periods of acceptance and rejection there can be no security, but rather a deepening insecurity for which some recourse must be sought elsewhere.

The permutations and combinations of these areas of parental activity show the variety of childhood experiences which are the inevitable consequences of growing up. Each child finds himself at some place in each scale, at some time of the day or night. And gradually, out of the repetition, the satisfactions, frustrations, changes, and interchanges there emerges his concept of justice. At first there are only faint glimmerings, but as he classifies, anticipates, corrects, and meditates, the necessity for finding an explanation for the code he eventually forms becomes a source first of insecurity and later of security.

The importance of the establishment of sound immature dependent security cannot be over-emphasized. Although wary of analogies, I cannot resist comparing this security to the platform from which a child learns to dive into the water. A rickety, unsteady, swinging board would make the early attempts not only ineffective but decidedly and unpleasantly fearful. However, a well anchored board gradually increasing in distance from the water provides an ideal platform from which to leap into adventure. In this fashion immature dependent security functions for the child's excursions into the unfamiliar. In the next chapter the dangers of too-cautious and too-cavalier treatment of the unfamiliar will be explored. For the present it can be stated that the best insurance against a later mental illness is an early and sound security pattern with its accompanying feeling of serenity.

5 · Insecurity

In which from boredom and resentment the appetite of change is shown to operate, producing insecurity, the patterns for dealing with which are learned. In which it is shown that insecurity may be the result of choice or may be thrust upon one, and that it is the basis of learning.

IT IS NO WONDER that parents of young children are often mystified and confused. Their child may be compared to an amateur juggler learning to keep three Indian clubs in the air at one time while standing on a raft floating on the backs of a group of performing seals.

The clubs represent three of the streams of the developmental process going on in the child: *emancipation, regression,* and *fixation.* These may be readily identified at birth, but can be described more accurately as time goes on. Emancipation is the desire of a child to get out from under the parental roof and control; regression is the tendency to return to the refuge of the home when the outside world becomes inhospitable; fixation, as I use the term, means an inclination to stay put and venture no further.

Boredom is an important prelude to emancipation. The child becomes bored in his relationship with the agent, and surprisingly, the more consistent the agent is, the more the child will want to venture forth. Equally effective in his emancipating is the resentment that a child feels first towards any hampering of his movements and later towards any delay to the immediate gratification of his wants. Quite early in life he figuratively adopts the slogan, "Don't fence me in," to be followed very soon afterwards by, "I want what I want when I want it." The influence of boredom is emphasized in this chapter; the impact of authority will be discussed under the later section on "emancipation."

The state of insecurity which follows a child's efforts to "get out from under" is like a wobbly platform. His conscious experience has changed from one of serenity to one of confusion. Insecurity is the state of mind that accompanies a person's uncertainty as to the consequences of his decisions and his doubts of his willingness to accept the consequences, whatever they may be. The intensity of his insecurity is determined by the degree of his uncertainty and the depth of his doubt. His feelings, which later he will identify as anxiety, are a mixture of confusion, excitement, frustration, apprehension, anticipation, and "keyed-upness." These feelings are the exact opposite of the serenity that accompanies security.

The young healthy infant may seem at first to be amenable, docile, and amusing even though at times a nuisance, but there are already signs of change—mild rebellion, inexplicable reactions. There are periods in which the "nuisance" factor seems to predominate. What is happening? As before, the schedules are being followed, "love" and affection are being displayed, comfort and companionship afforded, all of the best plans are being followed, and yet, "he seems to want something else." The platform has begun to rock.

The puzzle is a real one. What more should a child desire than to be well cared for, to have his wants anticipated and gratified, to be protected from harm, and to be related to agents who are being as consistent as possible? One of the "built-in" regulators of living beings is operating. This is the appetite of change. *The child is bored!* (The Garden of Eden must have been incredibly boring.)

Boredom arises from repetition, constancy, sameness in anything, even pleasure. To overcome boredom there must be change, either in the outer surroundings or in the inner resources of imagination, invention, or fantasy. But young children have few if any of these inner resources. They have no imagination, they only know reality. Hence they must seek change in the world about them. They must go out, "run away," find something new every minute. At first the whole world is new, but soon they exhaust their immediate surroundings. No matter how skilful the agents are in entertaining the child, they soon repeat themselves, and at that moment the child is bored.

To overcome boredom he strikes out for himself. He has a do-it-yourself kit handy. He can change the auditory environment at will. A good lusty yell, apparently without reason (to the mother, that is), is a change, especially if it causes a flurry of solicitous attention. He listens to himself, and whether he realizes that he is the origin of the sound is immaterial. (I once saw, and heard, in a growing flock of chicks, a young cockerel utter his first tentative crow, sharp and clear. He stopped still, apparently astonished and delighted, and then suddenly affrightened, scampered away.)

Later on when he learns to do more, he will "run away from home." How many devices have been invented to prevent a youngster from roaming? The yearly toll of the city streets testify to their inadequacy. Continuous surveillance is the only answer. When they have grown up, of course, there is no answer, but this later pattern will be discussed later. However, unaware at the moment of anything but "newness," the child looks, listens, feels, tastes, and revels in the novelty. However, there is a bad fairy hovering about: *fear*. Anything that is new or unfamiliar is fear-inducing roughly in proportion to its newness. Fear is basically unpleasant, and so the first reaction of the child is to avoid the new, but if he can overcome this tendency—and boredom helps him to do so—then the situation is fascinating. The net result of his seeking beyond his borders is a double-barrelled experience.

Although the new is pleasing, it is also repelling. A conflict arises. What to do? A decision confronts him. To return to the old and tried place from which he came, comfortable, safe, and serene, *or* to stay and, whatever happens, take it on the chin? If the former choice is made, he regresses to his old, trusted, prepared position, ready for another foray—perhaps. If the latter choice is selected, he is insecure and his mental state is one of *anxiety*. Of all the conscious attributes of anxiety, boredom is not one of them.

The degree of newness which determines whether an infant will stay or regress is a matter of conjecture. Extreme novelty, especially when it appears suddenly, will undoubtedly encourage escape. How soon will he fare forth again? When he is sufficiently bored. A situation that is only slightly new will encourage him to continue enjoying the thrill and will also stimulate further exploration. In this fashion the early experiences of a child will set the stage for his early attitude toward insecurity. So this double-barrelled aspect of insecurity means a tendency to retreat if fear dominates the situation, or an inclination to stay and enjoy the novelty if the fear can be overcome or endured. Adventure is an early goal.

Here is one of the early experiences of insecurity. A child is about to take his first step. He stands erect, and although he is reasonably confident in his new stature gained by holding on to a chair or his mother's hand, he hesitates to launch himself into the unknown world, a foot and a half above his safe position on the floor, with nothing to hang on to. But the consequence of trying is free locomotion, no dependence upon anything but himself, an adventure in levitation. What will happen? He doesn't quite know. Can he take it? He is not sure and so he sits down! He is back in a secure position. He has already learned to control a tendency to fall over backwards. "Let's try again," and he pulls himself up. Oftentimes his parents, one supporting him and the other with arms outstretched some inches away, are his guides and mentors. This time he decides to take a chance. One foot out, gently propelled from behind, he takes the other foot off the ground. He is free and falls into his mother's or father's arms. He has done it! Valiantly he has accepted the challenge. Later on, when lured to a greater distance, he may and usually does fall over. This may discourage him for a time, but ultimately the insecurity becomes less and less as the skill increases and the risk lessens to the point where walking becomes commonplace. Then he must try running, jumping, tumbling, climbing, gliding, and flying—and now to the moon!

Such series of events, of shorter or longer duration, are repeated again and again in a lifetime; learning to ride a bicycle, skate, and dance; hovering over the spending of the first allowance; overcoming the reluctance to wear a new dress to school; calling for the first date; choosing a job; proposing marriage; buying a house; treating the first patient; pleading the first case—to mention just a few of a great number of potential decisions.

At the same time a pattern for dealing with insecurity is crystallizing. First comes the gathering of knowledge, the refining of the accuracy of anticipation of consequences, either formally at school, from books, travel, or observation, or more effectively through actual living experience. Second, through this living experience comes the ability to gauge one's own capacity to accept consequences. The more accurately the developing person learns to know himself, the more likely is he to develop good judgment and caution and also to take a chance when the goal is worthwhile.

The early insecurities of the infant and child are usual, normal, and frequent. Children seek, recoil, return to inspect, retreat, reappear, examine, explore, become alert and curious. Curiosity is a positive outcome of insecurity. All children learn to be curious. One of the goals of child training is to preserve and foster and develop curiosity. Sometimes success is achieved and the result is a poet, composer, researcher, novelist, dramatist, inventor—all interesting people. Sometimes these learned patterns, which are usually *unusual*, are turned in a direction disapproved of by the society in which a child lives.

This pattern is also learned. If the thrill of non-conformity outweighs the fear of "not belonging," the essence of delinquency is distilled.

In adults as in children it is axiomatic that the time elapsing between the first awareness of a problem that requires a decision, and the final resolution of the problem by acting on the decision, is always a period of insecurity, of anxiety. It may last a moment or continue indefinitely. If there is shilly-shallying in deciding, the anxiety becomes chronic and it is then called "worry."

Only when a decision is made and acted on does the anxiety end. The die is cast. Consequences ensue. The actor will now compare these consequences with those which he anticipated, In this fashion he refines his judgment. And he must either accept the consequences or try to avoid them.

Let us consider a few examples. James is a young husband with a young and growing family. He has been a bit bored with the routine of his job. He finds himself at the race-course. Should he bet or not? He knows little about the procedure, the horses, and least of all, the results, except, that if a horse wins and he has a "ticket" on it, he makes money, otherwise he loses. He is insecure obviously as soon as he thinks, "Shall I bet or not." If he has just come to admire the view and the exhibition of speeding horseflesh, he is not insecure because he can enjoy both without help or hindrance. But he has put himself into a quandary. "Two dollars won't break me"; "I can buy Jane and Jimmy Jr. a present with my winnings"; "I can eat an apple for my lunches if I lose"; and so on. And so he bets, and now his insecurity increases. He cannot get his money back once it passes through the wicket, and he can do nothing to further the efforts of "his" horse. He waits, and stews and sweats and then "They're off." Whether he wins or loses, another scenario of insecurity begins. Shall he try to double his winnings or recoup his loss? If he decides to go home and congratulate himself that he has learned something about racing, namely that *for him* the risk of loss is not worth the fun of watching and waiting, then this form of insecurity has been put in its place— until the next time. In the meantime, he has learned to some extent to form his own judgment of the value of experience.

Insecurity may arise in several ways; an individual may choose to be insecure by placing himself deliberately in an insecure position, or he may not choose to be insecure; insecurity may be thrust upon him by accident or miscalculation. John is a mountain climber. He deliberately places himself in a position of insecurity. He trusts his skill and knowledge against a quantity of unknown factors. The thrill is fascinating. Part of the reward of success, aside from achievement itself, is the retelling of the exploit. If John is unsuccessful, the thrill is enhanced for those who later on accept the same challenge. At any rate, the insecurity is willingly accepted. This is an example of insecurity by choice.

However insecurity may be thrust upon a person by such episodes as loss of a parent, serious injury or illness, physical disasters such as floods, fire, war: all classified as *crises*. They cannot always be anticipated or controlled. The insecurity is suddenly and dramatically experienced. The consequences are immediately imposed. How the person will react depends on the pattern already established. Children usually regress and seek the agent who has looked after their immature dependency. Some adults who have not matured act in a similar fashion. With adequate training a child may grow up to accept the consequences of crises with whatever mature help he may have at hand.

There are other types of insecurity which are thrust upon us. A young child inevitably falls in the course of his explorations. Falling is one of the basic fears from which one never wholly frees one's self. We can learn to "take it on the chin" with more and more experience. We can learn to place ourselves deliberately in a position from which falling is a threat, such as jumping, bicycling, or climbing. The chance of falling is always present. To many people an airplane ride is such an insecure experience that they choose the more sedentary forms of transportation. In these instances the individual chooses between thrill and escape. He resolves the conflict in terms of his own acceptable ratio between the gratification of the appetite for change and the experience of inescapable fear.

Another form of this type of insecurity is being "lost." Most children at one time or another wander too far from familiar ground. Their reaction to this experience depends on a number of factors, but the principal feeling is one of loss of the dependent agent, the lack of knowledge of consequences, and the feeling of inadequacy. What to do? The anxiety increases in some instances to panic, which decreases effectiveness of action. Again, according to the training, the insecurity of being "lost" may be capitalized on by explorers to provide themselves with the thrill of adventure: on to the Amazon, darkest Africa, the poles, the moon, Mars, infinity!

Fires and floods and famine provide a further source of inevitable insecurity. The degree of insecurity is usually determined by the ineffectiveness of one's efforts employed to allay the disaster. Further, there are the disasters that are brought upon us by human social development, stock-market crashes, war and revolution. In each such disaster there is an element of thrill that makes reasonable control a difficult matter.

Even though insecurity is thrust upon a person unexpectedly, there is always an effective training programme which helps a child to accept such experiences. Grief, disappointment, failure, humiliation, rebuff, can be accepted with some good grace. The fact that they may be accepted without panic or hysteria does not indicate that the individual may not feel deeply. In these instances an agent such as mother, father, friend, husband, wife, is an indispensable solace.

It has become apparent that only through insecurity can one learn. The state of insecurity therefore must not be considered as either a malevolent experience or a benevolent one. Its value depends on how the individual deals with it. He may regress and remain fixed at an earlier stage, or he may forge ahead to self-dependence by accepting the challenge of the insecure state and expending his efforts to further learning.

In fact, the willingness to accept insecurity as an inevitable part of emancipation in its broader sense, to be anxious, to doubt, to be uncertain and like it, and finally to resolve all these difficulties by some considered action, this is the true signature of maturity and mental health. One must however be willing to accept the consequences. Of such stuff are moulded the successful executive, surgeon, general, and researcher. In such positions intelligence is important, but the acceptance of insecurity is imperative.

A person who has learned to accept insecurity willingly, and to accept the consequences thereof equally willingly, has acquired one of the techniques for building mental health. The two "acceptances" go hand in hand. There are many adults who are willing to be insecure provided someone bails them out if things get too hectic. Foolhardiness and bravado are generated when the rescue squad is too handy and too expeditious. Young children, of course, count on a rescuer. It is always a problem for the parent to decide when to rescue a child and when to stay in the background. One must safeguard him as best one can against serious injuries and then leave well enough alone. Many a mother, at the annual school games, endures the agonies of Milton's doomed while watching her young in the boxing ring. Yet each child must learn the hard way. For the first two decades of our lives, but with decreasing urgency, each one of us needs an agent to care for his immature dependency. We gradually emancipate ourselves from such agents with many a painful pang—on both sides.

Learning to accept insecurity and its aftermaths has many rewards.

However many facts a person may gather in a quest for knowledge, however many A's at examinations, or prizes for this and that, the mode of *application* of his knowledge determines whether he is a mentally healthy person or not.

The more risks he takes the more likely is he to be in the forefront of attention for a time. But unless he is willing to accept the consequences of a risk gone wrong, he falls by the wayside. (Whatever happens to the president of the freshman class?) The more willing he is to accept consequences, the more likely he is to assume more and more responsible positions. The successful executive is not necessarily the most intelligent, nor the most charming. He is usually one who has gradually learned to accept calculated risks and then make them turn out more often than not to be "justified." The astronauts are mature fliers in the third and fourth decade of their lives; the pilots that saved England (and others) in the battle of Britain were in their second and early third decades. The former are required to do a most demanding and responsible task, the latter were deliberately exploited for their willingness to risk everything, throw caution to the winds, for a more or less momentary experience of exhilarating insecurity. Both the stunt flier and the pilot of a jetliner accept insecurity, but the ways in which they deal with it differ. Likewise, a dictator's method of dealing with his insecurity is completely different from that of the squire of a peaceful, settled community. There are many critics in all communities who criticize the "do-nothings" of those in charge, confident in their own knowledge and competence. They lack only the necessity to accept the consequences of the plans which they never have to put into operation. It is so easy to be in the opposition.

Any attempt to protect a child from all insecurity (fortunately an impossible goal) would lead to his stagnation. There is, however, no rule of thumb. Each of us has a private limit to the novelty he can comfortably take in any specific area. We may be lions in our homes and sheep in the marketplace, or vice versa.

It must have occurred to the reader that not only the child is on an unsteady platform but so also are his parents. Each one is the product of a unique and personal programme of emancipation, regression, and fixation. Although there are common elements, no two such programmes are identical. So the parents' interpretation of their child's behaviour is complicated by their own patterns, goals (some fulfilled, some not), urges, and insecurities, among other things. It is fortunate that the human mind is such an excellent computer, even though it too makes mistakes.

6 · Emancipation and Regression

In which emancipation *is shown to be a form of active progress towards maturity, stimulated by the inevitable boredom and resentment of authority inherent in a sound family atmosphere. In which a feeling of belonging is shown to derive from a consistent immature dependency; and* regression, *a salutary process in childhood, is shown to be a mechanism which provides a safeguard from too vigorous and venturesome exploration. In which it is shown that* crises *are inevitable and can lead to more effective emancipation.*

ONE DAY in the late spring I watched a parent bird push a well-grown fledgling from the nest. It fluttered to the lawn, stood still for a moment, and then flew to the lower limits of a nearby lilac bush. From then on, it was on its own.

Later, in the early summer, I watched a mother put her young child into a playpen on the lawn outside the kitchen window. Then, with many a backward glance, she returned to the house. Her face appeared dimly at the window. The child's first reaction was to look around, then he appeared to miss his mother and burst into tears. The mother remained hidden, and in a few moments the child became interested in his new environment, and his old and familiar toys. The apron strings were stretching.

In the early autumn I saw a little boy trudge off to his country school for the first time. He did not look back. His mother had given him a parting embrace, shed a few tears silently in the warm, cozy, lonely farm kitchen. Symbolically, she untied her apron then and went outside to finish some of her chores. A much longer time would elapse before *he* would be "on his own."

On the other hand, one often sees young children in charge of toddlers on many streets (not just in slums), "on their own" long before they have reached a comparable stage of development to that of the ejected fledgling. Emancipation has been thrust upon them. They have been forced to accept responsibility long before they were able to handle it. This developmental anachronism is one of the contributory causes of delinquency. It is a false emancipation, giving the appearance of early sophistication.

Compared to other animals, the human infant is born very young, that is, at a very immature stage of his development. In our western society he is considered an infant (legally) until he is 21 years old. During this period he is said to be emancipating or maturing. What does this mean? According to our theory, he is gradually replacing his dependence upon his first agent and substituting other means of gaining and maintaining security and serenity.

Emancipation

Emancipation begins early in life. The first breath accompanies the infant's first cry of independence and is among his first wholly independent acts in his new world of experience. From then on the progress towards emancipation will proceed at varying rates with many setbacks (regression) and many static periods (which I have called fixation).

It must not be considered, however, that emancipation is a passive phenomenon which proceeds on its own. Although there are some biological components of maturation, such as growth in size, the conscious aspects of the programme are contributed by the efforts of the individual himself. He "works" at it. This necessity of effort on the part of the child is often overlooked. One hears an adult comment, "He is old enough to know better," as if emancipation were the result of an automatic process, part of growth, wholly independent of effort on the part of a child. One could as reasonably say, "He is old enough to play a violin. Let's hear a tune."

Because the whole process is spread over twenty years or more, it does not at first glance appear to be a learning programme. Yet it represents the most significant educational experience of all. A child is offered many adult examples of emancipation, mostly haphazard and informal, and he must choose whether to imitate or shun them.

Formal courses are occasionally offered whose precepts are belied by the social milieu in which the child grows up. Sunday schools, clubs, organized groups such as Cubs, Guides, and Scouts, and later service clubs and adult religious groups are all designed to assist the family in directing the emancipation of its children. In many cases, the very nature and goal of the organization tends to prolong dependency and immaturity because emancipation is looked upon as a form of "throwing off the yoke," "seeking freedom," or declaring "Give me liberty . . . ," whereas successful emancipation implies the voluntary acceptance of greater *restriction* upon free action than in the previous state of dependence. Self-control is substituted for outside control and self-indulgence. This misunderstanding of the nature of freedom is amply and tragically illustrated in the pangs of emancipation experienced by the emerging nations in Africa.

The goals of an infant, as already indicated, are projected into the immediate future. Gradually they are projected further and further. At first an infant wants everything that comes within his conscious ken. Then he begins to compromise; he gives up the moon for fireworks. Later he tries to get what he wants by fair means or foul, but he finds that he also wants to belong, and hence must curtail his brigandage. Once he discovers that there is more in life than success, a code emerges which determines his ultimate goal. At maturity, the adult projects a goal which is a product of his sense of social responsibility and his appreciation of purpose in living. Based on this sense and this appreciation, his code of behaviour further restricts his tendency toward immature self-indulgence.

Parents thus have a three-fold responsibility towards their children: to arrange for their survival; to teach them "know-how"; and, most important of all, to see that they learn to use their "know-how" to reach their *own* ultimate goals.

The last of these responsibilities is also the most difficult to carry out. It is self-evident that parents deserve all the help that may be offered. In the two areas of survival and know-how, the community, which is really a group made up mostly of parents, forms a concerted plan to become more effective. It administers public health programmes, public schools, public playgrounds. As for the code, there is still ample opportunity for expansion, especially by means of example set by the parents themselves.

The importance of an effective agent to care for one's immature dependency has been stressed; now the inevitability and advisability of getting rid of this agent will be discussed. This process of emancipation requires the effort of both the child *and* the agent, the one to break away gradually, the other to prevent too precipitate or too reluctant a break by providing an opportunity for the child to learn how to deal with his new frontiers.

The two basic motives which direct a child towards emancipation are those which we have already mentioned, boredom and resentment of restrictive barriers. They both operate from birth. The former begins to crystallize earlier, as indicated by the appearance of curiosity; the latter comes to fruition later when the child recognizes such sources of restriction as authority imposed from without.

Boredom

We have already observed the prominent causes of boredom. Now let us examine the child's development under its influence. Throughout his life a person attempts to escape boredom by seeking ever more distant fields, each greener than the last. One of the tasks of the agent on whom a child depends is to protect him from wandering too far off. When such control is exercised, a child's boredom and resentment of authority supplement each other.

As soon as he learns how to deal with the ordinary hazards of exploration without serious consequences, and how to find the way back home, he is given more leeway until ultimately he can assume full responsibility. When is this final stage reached? Perhaps when he learns to avoid all enterprises that do not require someone else to bail him out, figuratively and literally. But would not such a plan eliminate all adventure? No, because adventure of a secure nature is based on the calculated risk which implies a willingness to accept the consequences without the explicit promise of rescue. Columbus, Hudson, Marco Polo, and, closer home, Lindbergh and the astronauts, have exemplified this trait. Strangely enough, the more skill, knowledge, and willingness to accept the consequences, the more exciting the adventure.

The success of the family group in establishing a familiar, cozy, warm, affectionate, and understanding atmosphere increases the likelihood that the very consistency of such a pattern will induce boredom. Parents can be exciting, but thereby they sacrifice to some degree their role as dependent agents. Occasionally they "break down," much to the astonishment and consternation of their children.

For a child, parents, as human beings, gradually replace *things* as effective dependent agents. They can *come* to the rescue. They respond in a active manner, as sticks and stones and bricks and mortar cannot. They can contribute most to the feeling of *belonging*: a complex of many conscious experiences serving principally as a social buffer against the encroachment of fear. To venture beyond this human defensive barricade takes more courage (acceptance of consequences) than to leave behind familiar objects, but the rewards are greater because new humans are more exciting than the old toys, beds, and back gardens.

Within the family group a child establishes a position, or status, which he must learn to maintain and not take for granted. Seeking to get what he wants (reach his goals) a child sizes up each member of the family as a source of gratification. This interpretation of human behaviour gives a picture of "selfishness" which may seem unflattering. However, to interpret all behaviour as an attempt to gratify wants presents a more honest view than to try to distinguish between selfish and unselfish behaviour. According to our interpretation there is no such thing as *un*selfish behaviour. After all, one always tries to get what one wants. This continuous ferment, not necessarily vigorous or vindictive, is most complicated because it involves the interaction of each member of the family with each other and with the group as a whole. Yet it is precisely this interaction which refines the differences in personality. This was shown by our observation of the Dionne Quintuplets during their first five years. At birth they were almost identical in physical and intellectual capacities, but they gradually acquired wide differences in personality traits, diverging further with each succeeding year. Such differentiation in personality reflects upon the status of the person within the family. And as I have said, the more static and satisfying his situation, the more likely a child is to look further afield. It is when a child is willing to accept the consequences of meeting new people, that he is truly beginning to emancipate himself from family dominance.

All new things are fear-inducing. People particularly so, because it is so difficult to predict what they may do. This is the origin of xenophobia, but it also makes them so potentially fascinating. In dealing with other people, children must use whatever successful patterns they have learned within the family group. Often they find people outside the family circle reacting differently if not disappointingly to their approaches. But they nevertheless begin learning to emancipate themselves from the family. They forge new bonds of loyalty, seeking to belong to another group. Parents who are themselves secure in their relationships foster this venture on the part of their children; those who are insecure try to interfere with it.

A child's boredom is not an indictment of a family. Parents who are taken for granted are usually most successful in furthering emancipation. (Mothers who cry at their children's weddings may be shedding tears of relief.)

We now come to the second factor motivating emancipation: resentment against authority. A child at birth already shows an antagonistic response to the use of force. The antagonism increases in vigour as a child grows stronger. He resents manipulation; he resists being *put* in the bath but will enjoy swimming in a pool. Later he will resent and try to circumvent any restriction of his free movement toward his immediate goal. "No" is usually included among the first words he learns. This resistance to obstacles of any kind in his path is a salutary instinctive pattern. Persistent attack at problems is an essential attribute of effective learning. It is labelled a "strong will" in our own children, "obstinacy" in the children of others.

As a child reacts against restrictions he will discover that they are of two kinds: one is the obvious thwarting of endeavour ("Someone is always interfering with me"; "Whenever I want something either it is taken away or I am taken away"). This is later identified as "authority," and is personified in an adult. The second type of restriction, recognized much later, is that of his own inadequacy. He discovers that his attempts at changing the world to reach his goals are unsuccessful. He builds his blocks higher and higher only to have them fall over before he has finished his edifice. He discovers a pencil will not draw the picture he has in mind. He learns that the inhibition of these efforts is identified with *himself*, that it results from his own inadequacy. He reacts to both kinds of restriction in the same way. He may have a temper tantrum, which works successfully at times against outer restriction but never against his own inadequacy.

In both cases his first reaction is to get rid of all restrictions. If he could talk at this early age he would say, "Away with all rules and regulations and routines and schedules—let me climb ladders and stairs and light matches and cut my food and pour my milk—and get out of my way—and stay out." Perhaps it's forunate that he can't talk!

Depending upon the consistency and the degree of leniency or strictness with which discipline is administered by his agents, a child will formulate his own attitudes toward this type of authority. Emancipation is attained by accepting the necessity for some kind of regulation. He begins to make his own rules, later to be expressed as a "code" which has various names—code of honour, morals, or ethics—and which he will accept under his own terms and either follow or not. The governing factor will be the strength of his desire to belong to a group. Later he will accept the code of the group from which he wants acceptance. Thus he passes through a stage of militant emancipation from parental authority to accept self-imposed inhibitions which are often much more rigorous than those of what he imagined was his early servitude.

His reaction against the second type of restriction, namely his own inadequacy, consists of a persistent attack on the obstacles preventing him from reaching his goals. If this expenditure of effort results in learning, in acquiring skill and know-how, he reaches effective emancipation because "knowledge makes him free." Now he can choose the goals he wants, judge how much effort it will require to attain them, and then decide whether it is worth while to proceed. He is free to decide and then take the consequences. His goals will reflect his competence, and his competence will always increase with effort. Thus ambition will be his servant and never his master. Emancipation, indeed!

Regression

When the child in the process of emancipation steps out into a new world and finds that the fear induced by the unfamiliar outweighs the pleasure in the novelty, he will return to the security and serenity of his familiar and solicitous dependency. This is an act of *regression*, and must be considered a choice on the part of the child. He might have chosen to remain insecure, anxious, and exhilarated. The degree of newness that he can endure without regressing becomes a part of his personality. In childhood, especially in the early years, regression under certain circumstances is salutary and should be recognized as an important act in the process leading to eventual emancipation. The ratio between fear and adventure in a new situation depends chiefly on the degree of unfamiliarity or suddenness of the presentation of the new experience, the skills already learned, the certainty of being accepted in the "old" environment, and the ease with which the escape route may be traversed.

The unexpected is unfamiliar, but a familiar object, person, or phenomenon suddenly encountered also arouses fear. One requires time to identify and classify each experience. After recognition, an object falls into its familiar place, and one carries on as before. During the momentary fear there is a tendency to escape and return to safety, that is, to the care of the agent. The opportunity to regress under these circumstances is a salutary outlet since it prevents panic.

Even though a child is in a situation that is not potentially dangerous, he may not have acquired sufficient skill to deal with the problems that arise. The newness wears off, but he is unable to effect the changes necessary to maintain interest, and so after a momentary thrill he returns to the familiar fields. Confident of his status there, he is always certain that he will be welcome because he has never been disappointed. Finally, to the best of his knowledge the escape route has been kept open. Figuratively he had blazed a trail from his familiar haunts by which he could find his way back. Only when he is fully emancipated will he cut loose and like Columbus trust to his skills alone to bring him back—if return is possible.

In throwing off the restrictions of authority, regression plays a complementary role to emancipation. Having run away from home he has escaped rules and regulations, but with so few skills he finds he needs direction, advice, and control. Instead of waiting for him to run away, his parents need a plan of discipline which gradually requires him to assume more and more responsibility for his actions. Such a plan is the most difficult but exciting of parental duties and privileges.

The final step in accepting authority as a necessary part of growing up consists in assuming authority, in turn, over a group of others: supervising younger siblings, baby-sitting, assuming leadership in formal groups such as the Cubs and Guides, and eventually taking executive positions in business, politics, education, and the professions. Only through some provision for adequately supervised group contacts *outside* the family circle—nursery school, public school, community groups formal and informal—can this aspect of emancipation be effectively arranged. Siblings, like patriotism, are not enough. Once in a position of authority, one inevitably encounters criticism. Mature acceptance of it is an indication of growth. At every step there may be errors in judgment, but there need never be regression after the early years of apprenticeship are over. In the early years, being backed up by a higher authority generates loyalty. Loyalty will later be a necessary constituent of the more mature relationships which are discussed later on.

Loneliness

Fear is a frequent experience of the young. Everything new and unfamiliar arouses fear of shorter or longer duration. Therefore, there is a tendency to hold hard to a familiar solace and refuge. Inanimate objects serve to some extent as such a refuge. A child will cling to a blanket, a wooden sword, a dismembered old and familiar doll, an old pipe, bedroom slippers, a dressing gown, or a trinket; but very early in life, human companionship is given first place. To have at hand a familiar person is the prime asset of childhood. The comfort of belonging stems from the feeling of serenity that accompanies the dissipation of fear when one is surrounded by or enfolded within the "bosom" of a family, the clan, or the gang. The very use of the term "bosom" indicates the derivation from the early maternal embrace and its effective contribution to the experience of belonging.

Recently, however, there has been an over-emphasis on the desirability of group living; the necessity for privacy is often neglected. Only when a child or adult is alone can he do concentrated, original and creative thinking. Privacy is a precious and significant privilege. Privacy, the sanctity of isolation, has long been taken for granted as a part of freedom but it is seldom stressed in an educational programme. So much emphasis has been placed upon "togetherness," which should not be confused with "belonging" as used in this book, that the opportunity for privacy is gradually being whittled away. Each move toward the modern way of living has reduced the opportunity for privacy. Little by little, small apartments (indeed, one-room apartments); the telephone, radio, and TV; the advertising camel; biased news channels; propaganda machinery of all kinds; conformity cults—all these make privacy not only difficult but rather suspect.

Although the obvious solution for a person who is lonely would be to seek companionship, preferably with his familiars, this may be a regressive measure—an opportunity to escape from one's self. At times such escape is salutary. At other times it is necessary to accept aloneness. In order to do so one must have increasing skill in changing one's inner world. If loneliness is thus accepted, time is often too short to complete a task before the demands of sociability impinge on privacy.

During our supervision of the young Dionne Quintuplets at Callander, we had arranged a small room equipped with chair, table, books, and toys to which one of the sisters could be confined as a disciplinary procedure. Quite frequently we would find that one of the five had isolated herself in this room, and was fully and happily occupied. All nursery schools should provide space for privacy. What has been called "isolation" is essentially a form of consolation, a privilege which has been much misinterpreted.

Crises

In the march towards complete emancipation there may be occasions when a problem is presented which is far beyond the capacity or ability of a child to solve. Such times are called crises. They occur when one finds oneself lost; is disabled by illness or accident; loses a close companion, especially a mother; or, later on, loses one's fortune, position, status, or esteem.

It is difficult to prepare for a crisis, although some crises may be softened in effect by a regressive formula such as insurance. But there is no insurance against grief. Self-control is the only safeguard against the impact of a sudden and unexpected blow. But during the period it takes to acquire self-control, regression is a safe and salutary method for relief. A child seeks his mother when hurt, a youth in defeat seeks the sympathy of his comrades, an adult in despair seeks the companionship of a close friend. Thus, depending upon how serious the crisis, some form of regression may remain as a recompense for the impossibility of achieving complete independent security.

In early childhood, the most frequent crises are those which arise through illness and accident, especially if these are followed by some form of incapacity. The next most frequent are disappointments caused by postponed or cancelled "fiestas."

Fortunately, many disabling and crippling illnesses have been greatly reduced in extent, but others still remain. Helping a young child to accept the consequences of the restrictions imposed by a disability places a huge burden upon his parents and teachers. To play the role of teacher and taskmaster on the one hand and sympathetic mother or father on the other calls for a high degree of courage and patience, and a great deal of security that is not uncommonly found. Only the failures are called to our attention. The natural response of adults is frequently to accept the regression of handicapped children. Yet their emancipation from immature dependency is essential for the acquisition of independent security and of mature dependent security.

The Goal of Emancipation

What is the end point of emancipation? How can one identify it? Final emancipation is achieved by the child's gradual withdrawal from parental authority. When it is reached, parents no longer have any authoritative part in the lives of their adult children. All decisions of the children are made uninfluenced by parental guidance; such independence is in accordance with or in spite of their teaching. Indeed, when emancipation is completed, the parents are spectators of their children's lives.

Does this imply a cutting off of all relationship? No, only the severing of parental authority. The parents may remain in their roles as authorities only insofar as they can offer information. In making decisions, the grown child must go to some outside source in order to fill in gaps in his own knowledge and to predict consequences. The parent, with his wealth of experience, may be the person to whom he turns. The parent will try to outline the consequences of various choices of action in the situation under discussion. But the child now must be free to accept or reject the information on the basis of its pertinence and significance to him. Such an ideal relationship would be most successful, since it would be based on mutual trust. However, it is quite rare to find a relationship which is free from dominance on the one side and of dependence on the other.

What is the desirable residue in this parent-child relationship? What remains of the two decades of parental care, training, solicitude, and ambition? Ideally, the successful emancipation of children results for the parents in:

1. a sense of fulfilment in a job well done;
2. pride in the achievement of a successful programme now ended;
3. relief after a long period of gradually lessening responsibility;
4. a remaining companionship, with no demands on either side.

For the child emancipation results in:

1. a deep respect which grows every year as he realizes what a task the raising of children really is;
2. a feeling of achievement at having participated in a splendid project;
3. a deep humility as he gradually realizes how much was contributed without actual appreciation on his part;
4. a recognition that the debt can only be repaid by his similar contribution to the next generation.

Any departure from this ideal is a sign that emancipation is incomplete.

The most difficult art to master is the art of training one's own children. To balance the urgency of youth to "fly away" against the responsibility of adulthood to safeguard health, both physical and mental; to stand aside in silent anguish and watch a child make mistakes that he must correct himself; to offer solace only when it is sought and to avoid the temptation of encouraging his return to childhood—these are only a few of the pitfalls of parental experience. There are many compensations. A child successfully trained is the most difficult, the most rewarding, and the most eloquent handiwork of man.

7 · Independent Security

In which it is shown that independent security derives from the acceptance of the challenge of boredom and arbitrary authority, is achieved through the expenditure of effort, and proceeds from primitive to mature patterns. In which the origin of the concept of justice, the place of gambling, competitive sports, and aesthetics, and the limits of self-confidence are defined.

A PERSON who is willing to accept the consequences of his actions without trying to avoid them in any way and without depending upon anyone to accept them for him is said to be *independently secure.* Serenity is the conscious component of this state, as it is of all secure states. Independent security can only be attained by first being insecure, by accepting the challenge of the insecurity and expending effort to deal with it. Thereby one acquires skill and knowledge which lead to independence. Skill and knowledge make it easier to predict and therefore accept consequences, and hence pave the way to further effort. One cannot inherit the state of independent security, or achieve it by any short-cut method, in spite of the alluring and lurid advertisements to the contrary.

This state of mind should not be confused with the feeling of "safety." Safety is the antithesis of independent security. An independently secure person is willing to meet the challenge of living without the protective armour of an agent. He has become his own agent by acquiring self-confidence and self-reliance. He now places his trust in himself.

To seek safety is to seek an agent. It is to adopt armour of various kinds, barricades, body-guards, and other similar devices, all of which are vulnerable. An independently secure person depends upon his skill, knowledge, and self-confidence to meet and solve problems, if not triumphantly, at any rate vigorously. Failure is one of the consequences which he must learn to accept in a mature fashion.

In childhood and early adult life, independent security is relatively rare, as would be expected. A false front often hides the insecurity behind it, not only from others but also from oneself. An individual who has acquired a degree of independent security is basically dynamic and will accept the necessary preceding state of insecurity with verve and mild excitement. Then when the problem has been examined and the solution arranged, he proceeds with self-confidence to carry it out. A skilled craftsman, surgeon, or engineer carries on his work calmly, ready for the unusual if it should appear, confident that he can deal with it. He is serene. At night he can sleep.

As indicated in the previous chapter, there are two main challenges that move an immature dependently secure person to become insecure: boredom and the restriction of arbitrary authority; and these also move him to independence. There are ways of relieving insecurity which will be discussed in another place. They include the maintenance of status, the necessity to "belong," the drive for self-preservation, and the development of loyalties. The discussion of boredom and restriction at this time will serve to indicate how independent security is attained.

Boredom

A person who is bored seeks a change. As we have seen, an infant becomes restless because this is the only way he knows how to change his world. Later his restlessness, now more expansive because he has learned to grasp objects, bang and throw them, and yell more loudly, becomes more exciting to him. Excitement, noise, energetic movement —these are the ingredients any immature person uses to relieve boredom. A New Year's Eve celebration indicates how long this pattern persists. There is an element of independence in this, but there is also a large residue of immature dependence in that the revellers are not willing to accept the restrictions of community living, namely the consideration for others. Vandalism and leaderless mob action are the adult expression of this primitive attempt at independence. At any rate the "leaders" of mobs are seldom in the forefront and often indeed are very far behind.

In its early states in young children the pattern of excitement, noise, and movement represents inexperience and lack of skill; in adults it represents a regression to infantile methods of solving problems.

The urge to find a change is recognized as *curiosity*. One who is bored seeks change and is gratified; but if the change is too marked it generates fear and hence causes him to retreat. Advances and retreats are the essence of curiosity. Thus a person is not *born* curious, but he is born with the two motives: appetite for change and capacity for fear. When he is older his curiosity will show itself in the amount of change he can take before he becomes afraid and desires to escape. The more independently secure a person becomes, the more new and unfamiliar situations he can accept. Fear is not necessarily eliminated altogether, but it has become tolerable. In this fashion, the spirit of adventure is generated.

One must distinguish between the behaviour of a child who is adventurous and that of an adult adventurer. The adventurous child is often foolhardy; he does not recognize the risks and he expects his immature agent to accept the consequences for him. The independent mature adventurer is one who calculates the risks and is willing to pit his skill against them and accept the consequences himself.

The gradual acceptance of fear as an essential element of insecurity leads to a more mature method of dealing with boredom: curiosity will now be directed toward solving problems. The situations that rise from seeking new experience will be analysed and stated in the form of questions. A person asking a question is insecure, but in seeking the answer he is starting on the road to independence. Of course each answer poses a further question, so that total independence can never be reached.

To guess at the earliest questions which a child poses for himself is a fascinating task. The chart in Chapter 2 represents my own guess. The developmental sequence is assumed to progress through the questions: *Which? When? Where? What? Who? How? Why?* This series of questions covers a period of approximately the first nine years of a child's mental age. There is inevitably a wide variation in the chronological age at which children ask such questions. There is also a great deal of overlapping, and the order may be interchanged. The only question which is undoubtedly in its proper place is the last. *Why?* means, "What is the purpose of life, the universe, anything?"

Asking questions is one of the early signs of growing independent security. It is a method deliberately employed in educational settings to teach by proposing problems and seeking the answers. "If you have two apples and I give you two, how many apples would you have?" "How does water get up into the clouds?" "What is energy?" "How do you prove an answer to be correct?" "Are those unanswerable questions?" and so on.

Finding the answer always involves effort, however slight or vigorous. It also involves the use of hands and tools and all the muscles as well as ideas. Invention is the task of finding new answers to old questions. A project may take a few moments or may last a lifetime. A person who has acquired a habit of asking himself questions and seeking the answers thereto need never be bored.

Asking a question and seeking an answer is the *mature* way of relieving boredom, first, because the individual welcomes his insecurity and anxiety; second, because seeking the answer involves effort which is pleasant; and last, because the answer turns up something new, a change.

Antagonism against Authority

I have described how a person acquired likes and dislikes under the heading of "attitudes" in my earlier books. Here a special set of attitudes is introduced. Not only does a child respond directly to all sensory experiences, but if an outside force is applied to move a part of the body of an infant, such as the foot, fingers, or head, there is an immediate retaliation by the muscle group that opposes this movement. For example, if one tries to straighten out the fingers of a child's clenched hand, the fingers immediately close more tightly. This response pattern remains throughout life more or less modified in intensity. When one is standing in a queue, pressure from behind is immediately resisted. "No admittance" calls forth an urge to enter. "A chip on the shoulder," "save face," "national honour": these are all shorthand notes testifying the prevalence and persistence of this instinctive pattern. A child resents the restriction involved when adults take off and put on his clothes, for this activity represents the arbitrary use of force, however benevolent. Later on, schedules and routines are imposed which interfere with the free expression of his wants.

Still later, resistance and antagonism in some situations are invited and welcomed, as in such sports as football and hockey. Here the antagonists are willing to accept the consequences and deal with them without resentment, but the tiger is only under the skin. At times, resentment appears; a fight, a rumble, an altercation. This primitive and immature pattern of behaviour is relished by the spectator because they can enjoy vicariously the blood and thunder without having to accept any of the unpleasant consequences. Bullfights, professional boxing, and motor racing are still more primitive.

The crux of the matter lies in the fact that a child wants what he wants when he wants it. He will later interpret this experience in its most simple aspect as "freedom" and his desire to indulge himself generates the idea of "rights." A person will interpret as unwarranted any interference with his rights or his freedom. Presented with the problem of restricted gratification and required to find an answer, he will be insecure. The primitive and immature solution of rebellion, violence, or flight has persisted in adults to this day under the banners and placards of freedom and rights. In the past, might was accepted as right. Only recently has a more mature method of dealing with the problem been operative in practice, although it has been widespread in precept for centuries.

The mature method of dealing with restrictive authority involves a long learning programme. First must come the recognition that some regulation is an essential arrangement of social life, and second a code must be accepted for regulating human behaviour so as to ensure one's own goals, but not at the expense of others. This code must provide for both non-conformity and conformity in order that the individual may find compensation in the one to offset the restriction in the other. In this fashion "freedom" ceases to be licence and becomes voluntary control, and "rights" become privileges and responsibilities.

Through this learning programme, which in our western society is expected to take at least 21 years to complete, each person constructs his own idea of justice, based on his own experiences. The law is an interpretation of justice as expressed by individuals throughout the years. The courts are mistakenly thought of as courts of justice; they are in fact courts of law. That the administration of the law most frequently corresponds to what most people consider justice is beside the point. The law, of course, recognizes this distinction. In order to approximate justice and to administer the law, a court of equity was invented. In some countries an ombudsman is appointed to perform this task.

A person who achieves independent security will accept the necessity to control his wants in accordance to an accepted code of ethics. For example, if Canadians had been independently secure as a community, all that would have been necessary at the outbreak of war in 1940 was a radio notice by the Prime Minister advising all Canadians to confine their purchases of butter, meat, liquor, and other commodities to a rigid minimum, and each of us would have complied. We all know what happened. We were not independently secure, so ration cards, hoarding, black markets became expressions of our immaturity.

But let us return to our child, growing up in an atmosphere of authority. He cannot avoid coming into contact with authority because if he is to survive someone must look after him and control him in some fashion. The attempts to evaluate the effectiveness of authority leave a great deal to be desired. It is naive to talk about a broken home, a delinquent home, or a bad or good home. The evaluation must be made in terms of how the authority is administered. Is it strict or lenient, consistent or inconsistent, possessive or neglectful, rigid or flexible, and to what degree?

No one episode, but rather the accumulation of the continuous process of control determines a child's concept of justice. Either he will think of justice as a formula for mature living and will accept its advantages together with its restrictions, or he will think of it as a device for prolonging an unbearable servility to arbitrary and whimsical authority. The example of his elders will add confusion to his thinking. No wonder there is still widespread acceptance of vengeance as an acceptable retaliatory procedure.

There are several aspects of the progress toward independent security in the acceptance of authority to be considered. First there is the matter of gradually working out a formula to establish a ratio between conformity and non-conformity. A child may decide that conformity is comforting in itself. It may become an immature agent. The child who, in an extremely permissive school, asked his teacher in plaintive tones, "Do I have to do today, all day, what I want to do?" illustrates the point. Schoolboys boast of the rigidity of the discipline under which they tacitly enjoy life. Rules of sophisticated behaviour save much embarrassment. Protocol serves a very useful purpose; secret societies revel in artificial rules. A satisfactory degree of conformity makes possible adventure into non-conformity, provided that the conformity is self-imposed or willingly accepted. Unwillingly accepted conformity leads to rebellion. For twenty years a person has an opportunity of deciding whether it is worthwhile to accept laws, customs, and traditions in order to carry on in peace a degree of acceptable non-conformity. The orators in Hyde Park illustrate the point. They may "non-conform" within wide limits, but not beyond them.

Then there is the matter of ownership. When a child begins to ask himself "whose?" he finds it difficult to discover an answer. Fortunately he has a long time to seek. In the meantime, he will make many mistakes. He will take things that do not "belong" to him. How many solid tomes rest on the shelves of law libraries expounding the rules of private property ownership! And yet we often expect children of tender years not only to know the rules but also to obey them.

The independently secure person respects other peoples' possessions and the sanctity of their bodies and lives. But how much blood and ink has been spilled in order to establish the thin hairline between mine and thine? A young child just snatches and solves his problem by possession if possible. He resents any restriction on this mode of gratifying a want. Later when he learns that snatching is disapproved of, he becomes more secretive. He finds that this natural form of gratification is called stealing and is highly disapproved of, and that the consequences are usually unpleasant, if he is caught. There are many formulae for solving the problem of ownership. They range from communal societies where there is no private ownership, just trusteeship (even of tooth brushes?), through so-called socialist and welfare states, to societies in which there is rigid ownership of what one has inherited or acquired.

A child is often disconcerted on moving out of the closely-knit family group in which he has been living. The family has been a commune or "sharing-ship," with a good deal of communal ownership (such as beds, TV, chairs, dishes). A few odds and ends have been his own: his toys of the moment, his clothes until he grows out of them or finds them on his younger brother, his "collections." When he is just outside of the family he finds that ownership is stressed, particularly in its negative aspect. "This does *not* belong to you," he hears on every side. Having learned some of these rules and having accumulated some possessions, he is further puzzled as he grows older to discover that ownership has rather restricting limits. He does not *own* equally those things which he thinks belong to him. What he thinks he "owns" is subject to unnumerable threats—taxes, dues, interest rates, and by-laws. He must obey the laws of property in all their devious applications. Finally he learns that "he can't take it with him." If he comes through all of this and decides that property, personal and real, is not a possession, but a tool to help him get what he wants when he wants it within the framework of conformity, he will be accepted by the social group in which he lives; and if he finds that he can get what he wants without violating the code which he has imposed upon himself, then he is independently secure.

He will also learn that his thoughts are much freer than his actions. There are limits of course. He may find the concept of "infinity" hard to deal with as applied to space and time, though as a mathematical symbol it will have well-defined meanings. No one can control his thoughts, sometimes not even himself. He and others will sometimes try—to little avail. But his thoughts must not spill over into action if by so doing he breaks his code. To live within the code is the only real freedom he has. If he is willing to accept the consequences of exploring new ways of thinking and new conclusions he is truly free, and he is indeed independently secure.

The Importance of Effort: Learning

Man is never free from wanting. Whether he still wants what he wanted after he has obtained it is immaterial. He goes on wanting. At first most of a person's wants, closely derived from his needs, are gratified by an agent—sometimes before he recognizes them. Later on he finds that he must make some effort either to make his wants known or to obtain their gratification on his own. At first his wants, projected into the future, may be either vague or specific. After he has had more experience they become more clarified, They are called goals if he sets them up, or incentives if other people set them up for him. These may include sweets, companionship, a bicycle, a doll's house, a baseball, a job, a mate, a house, an elected post, or a million dollars.

The more specific the goal, the more likely he is to try some means other than restless activity to reach it. The English language is somewhat ambiguous about wants. One hears, "I often have to do what I don't *want* to do." This means that there are alternative wants and at times one must select among them. A young boy says "I'd rather go fishing than go to school," but he does go to school. At that moment, for many reasons, he chose to go to school, indicating that this was the dominating want of the moment. We never do what we do not want to do, except under duress. Even the mention of duress begs the question, for a choice made under duress is simply an expressed *want* for the least undesirable alternative.

Effort always involves some kind of muscular movement. "Pure" mental activity without muscle involvement is a myth. Concentration, for example, requires a definite muscular set. Try concentrating on a sunny summer afternoon, dozing in a hammock under the shade of a tree, and you will feel as exhausted as after a brisk run. Muscular activity is always accompanied by kinaesthesia, which is the conscious awareness of movement. This experience is perhaps the most intimate of the senses and is most readily identified with a notion of the "self" as it gradually emerges in the child's mind. Therefore, the expenditure of energy, of effort, is from the beginning an intimate experience, and so is all that is connected with effort. The need, the associated want, the context of the striving, the evaluation of the progress toward the goal are fused into a composite whole in which the sense of self is an important component. Sometimes there is a distortion of this process and the individual has a feeling of "unreality" as if the self were not included.

The expenditure of effort, whether desultory or rigidly directed, will be judged successful or not in terms of the extent to which it brings an individual closer to his goal. There will be setbacks (failures) and advances (successes). Final success will depend upon several factors: whether the want still continues, whether the goal is still desirable, whether the individual is capable of reaching it, and whether he has accumulated previously successful patterns of achievement He either keeps on trying or gives up—that is to say he succeeds or fails. Let us leave him here for a moment.

Everyone who has watched the young of any species will observe the apparent joy and delight which accompanies sheer movement: gambolling, running, jumping, climbing, rolling, usually accompanied by noise of some kind. The human species is no exception. When the gratification of a personal want is added to this joy of movement, it is easy to understand that expending effort towards a goal is one of the most pleasant and desirable of human experiences.

From this it follows that the more effort is expended the more a person's gratification is enhanced. Increased effort is required to overcome difficulties (which are intermittent failures), and more difficult tasks are more rewarding than easy ones. One may observe this by watching a young child learning to ride on a self-propelled three-wheeled cart. Having mastered the steering and the footwork, he seeks to make the task more difficult. He rides it backwards or kneeling and using only one foot for propelling, or trying with an infinite variety of arrangements to stand on his head. In just this fashion adults increase their difficulties in golf by placing traps in the most effective places for preventing low scores. Thus achieving becomes the important element in learning. The goal often recedes, "turns to ashes," as in British cricket. "Having achieved" has already become past history, but it is exceedingly important in its future reference. Having once succeeded, one is spurred on to accept a new challenge, and mindful of past success one keeps on trying. The "failures" have made life more interesting. One may conclude that persistent effort depends more on accepting failures than on achieving successes; there are certainly more of the former. It is by overcoming failures that one persists towards success, though one may merely encounter further failures.

Learning is far more complicated than it is generally considered to be. The process of getting a child to learn is commonly thought of as being like fastening a carrot in front of a donkey's eyes and applying some pressure from behind—the goal and the motive, the want and the need. Actually in between motive and goal, many factors are involved, including a change in the goal, the skill of the learner, and the anticipation of consequences.

One of the most common aspects of a learning process is the *change* which may take place in the goal. The goal may either increase or decrease in its appeal. For example: A child is building a rabbit hutch out of some old boards and wire. Halfway through his job he stops to reconsider. He is having fun, but he begins to ask himself whether the effort is worth while, if the fun he is having is depriving him of fun, for instance, of playing baseball. He is beginning to realize that the goal may be beyond his capacity. He is also tired. He gives up for the time being and leaves the half-finished hutch in the middle of the garden.

He has been told, "If you start something you must finish it. Don't clutter up the garden, the driveway, or the middle of the room with your stuff." So he puts it away, never to touch it again, or perhaps to take it out later and evaluate the whole matter again; or he may leave it to find later that someone else has disposed of it, causing him to give the project up for good. After all he didn't have any rabbits anyway.

Over a period of time a child discovers, sometimes with surprise, that his *skill* in a particular area has increased. He drives a nail more efficiently; he catches a ball more often; he spells more accurately; he rides his bicycle with more aplomb; he seems to know the correct answers to more questions. He is acquiring knowledge and know-how. His recognition of his achievement tends to make the undertaking of a new task easier and more stimulating.

Furthermore, he learns to *anticipate* the consequences of his actions, and therefore is in a position to accept them. He learns that his predictions are not always accurate, although his foresight improves with practice. But, more important, he finds that whether he is accurate in his predictions or not, he can accept the consequences without much ado and keep on towards his goal. Acceptance of consequences becomes a part of his personality. He finds that hindsight is better than foresight; that it is an important part of his accumulated knowledge.

Several such learning programmes running concurrently, both formally in school and informally in play, become the living patterns of development. One never stops learning, although the progress at times may defy detection. The longer one lives, the more efficiently can one learn, providing one keeps in practice. Children appear to learn more rapidly because they have·so much to learn. Selection becomes more and more essential as one grows older. Controversy is becoming more and more acute over what basic subjects should be learned—should they be reading, writing, and arithmetic? Most of the fuss and fury is contributed by those who have placed these three skills on pedestals which are far too high; and they are encouraged to elevate them even further by pseudoscientists who have a vested interest. We will not err in educating children if our central aim is to foster the development of curiosity and to keep alive the zest for learning as a means and not an end. It is apparent that everyone achieves some degree of skill in a number of areas; no one is successful in everything. The day of the universal genius is past, if it ever existed. Surely Aristotle, Erasmus, or Bacon did not know everything. Omniscience and omnipotence are denied to men. But one may achieve pre-eminence in one field or even a few fields in which one may be independently secure. The proof of achievement lies in one's resisting the temptation to assume a comparable status in an adjacent field because of one's prestige. A top-flight physicist is not necessarily an informed social philosopher.

Independent security is not a static state of mind. Its very nature suggests periods of inquiry (insecurity) which require further learning. In any vocation, serenity and security follow upon an apprenticeship, long or short. The excitement of learning, of achieving, of overcoming difficulties, of struggling to become more adept, more knowledgeable, more confident, is interspersed by periods of relaxation, rest, and serenity. Thus independent security is pursued.

Recently I heard a speaker, talking about retirement, say, "Nothing succeeds like your successor," which is an interesting paraphrase of the usual cliché. There is truth in the apparently flippant remark. Those who have reached the highest peak in their professions, art, or craft, are those who were concerned not with "beating" others but with doing a job well for their own satisfaction, and then passing on to their successors the benefits of their achievements as goals and examples. The teacher who sees his pupils gradually become more knowledgeable than himself enjoys the most gratifying achievement of all—he is truly serene.

Limits of Independent Security

It must be emphasized that the area of independent security is limited, and stops far short of omniscience and omnipotence. It ill betides anyone who either seeks these goals or, worse, thinks he has attained them. Some do!

The limits to the acquisition of independent security are quite easy to describe, but not to measure. First there is the capacity—both physical and mental—of the individual. But this is only an apparent limitation; providing one discovers it for oneself and accepts it, it does not interfere with developing independent security. A person of lower capacity can be as independently secure as a person whose capacity is higher. Trying to satisfy a vaulting ambition can deny security to both capable and less capable persons. "A man's reach should exceed his grasp," but not too far. When public exploitation of the differences in human abilities occurs only in areas that may be trivial, such as in games, hobbies, and racing, it does little harm. But when prizes and rewards are offered for achievement that arises out of individual initiative, then independence becomes more difficult to attain.

Time is another limiting factor which one must critically evaluate in terms of one's capacity. It is extremely difficult to judge whether an effort is worth the time spent on it, because it is so easy to give up if we can persuade ourselves that the effort would have been wasted. Self-evaluation (criticism) is an essential element of independence. Criticizing one's self is the prelude to accepting criticism from others. Unfortunately the criticism from others usually precedes one's own, and a bellicose attitude may develop towards all criticism.

Self-criticism may also be distorted in the other direction; it may become an excuse for not undertaking anything new and so may become an impediment to the growth of independent security.

Sport and Aesthetics

Some forms of behaviour which appear to manifest independent security may be basically outcomes of insecurity. Examples are found in sport and in the field of aesthetics. Whenever one competes with another person, whether the competition is on an individual or team basis, there can be no independent security, however much skill has been acquired, *unless one is indifferent to the final outcome of the game.*

Let us watch two people playing chess. Each pits his skill against the other, concentrating on his own plan, trying to discover his opponent's plan and circumvent it while furthering his own success. Some moves are familiar. Seldom, if ever, are two games alike. Uncertainty and insecurity are accepted, and the game is thrilling, exciting to the end. One or the other succeeds, or the game ends in a draw. A draw is the most gratifying result because it implies that each is a worthy opponent to the other. At any rate, the contest is over with. No triumph on the one hand, no humiliation on the other. No statistics are kept. It has been a period of change from other tasks, and this is what is important.

If the skill of one of the players is much greater than the skill of the other, the contest is displeasing to both: the one is bored, the other confused. *But* if the end result is important to either, then winning becomes important and losing is to be avoided at all cost. Hence the anxiety that prevails all through a "tight" game is not pleasant because the outcome always looms supreme. What a woeful sight to see the old alumni crushed after watching the team go down to defeat, and what an even more woeful sight to see them jubilant in victory!

When sport becomes a profession the picture changes. Calm, serene self-confidence is to be desired. The activity in the arena is no longer a game, it is bread and butter. But a player can never predict with complete accuracy what the consequences of his actions will be. There are too many variables. A failure is often catastrophic for the moment. A pitcher who is "taken out" has not lost his physical skill or endurance; he could pitch all afternoon in practice, but for the moment he has lost his self-confidence, and he is not given the opportunity to restore it. And so he goes to the showers, perhaps muttering, "I'll never give *him* another high and outside." He comes back in a few days and perhaps pitches a "no-hitter." A competent golfer in a contest may "blow up" for the same reason. He too learns from his "mistakes."

In professional football one seldom sees "dirty" acts (there may be the odd one that is missed), because they are dangerous and expensive. Such sports are exciting mainly for the spectators, who of course have no responsibility in the affair, and for the "backers" who are financially involved but who have their main skills in other areas.

What about gambling? Only the professional gambler can be independently secure because by some means or other he is usually betting on a sure thing or covering potential loss. The amateur never really anticipates losing because he thinks the odds are in his favour; otherwise he would be foolish to bet. But, then, he is never certain, hence the excitement. To pit one's knowledge, intuition, and hunches against the unknown and to prove one's self a prophet—what a thrill! Providing one is willing to accept the consequences, gambling is a diverting game, but as with the little boy and the scooter, the stakes have got to be made higher or it is not thrilling enough. Furthermore, one must not involve others in the gamble, because to do so forces them to accept consequences in whose arrangement they have had no part. Thus a husband and father must not gamble his weekly wages, for that involves his whole family.

Like sports, artistic creation makes use of insecurity to produce an ultimate state of independent security. Objective judgment of one's own achievements, a rare quality, is the basis of aesthetics. The independently secure person judges the merits of a painting, a musical score, a landscape, or even a "well-turned-out" person in terms of appreciation of the amount of effort which would be expended in creating it. This is the prime essence of beauty. How often does one hear this disparaging remark about a work of art, "I could do as well myself!" Later on the aesthetic quality is complicated by the desire for possession, which is largely a desire for maintaining or achieving status. Advertisers today, as always, in a large measure dictate taste. Awe, one of the components of aesthetic experience, is an acquired and sophisticated feeling. No young child experiences awe. But a person who has achieved some degree of competence in a related field appreciates the incredible effort required to produce the vaulted dome of St. Paul's Cathedral. How infinitely far it is from his own puny efforts. Perhaps he also feels fear because of the nearness of such power. Contemplation of the Grand Canyon, the Rocky Mountains, or the milky way results in the same feeling of awe, wonder, and exultation for something achieved by more than human effort.

Assets and Liabilities of Independent Security

And finally, there remains for the truly independently secure person the memory of the thrill of combat or effort in solving problems, overcoming difficulties, accepting disappointment and frustration, followed by the serenity of accomplishment for its own sake. There is no triumph in such achievement, for triumph suggests victory over an adversary. Competition has no place; only co-operation, assistance, and generosity. Triumph is upsetting. If a record is made, it will be broken. Every record ever made has been superseded—except the latest, and it waits its turn.

But there is a price to be paid for independence—loneliness. The captain of the ship at sea is a lonely person. The acceptance of responsibility implies self-confidence, trust, and faith in one's self. It is fortunate that independent security can never become absolute. There is always a place for a helper.

8 · Mature Dependent Security

In which it is shown that emancipation proceeds faster than the acquisition of independent security; that the human being is not social by nature, but becomes so as he finds human beings gratify his wants; that to fill his security needs, he forms mature dependencies; that these consist of mutual relationships and the acceptance of an over-all authority.

FOR A SHORT TIME after birth, a child under adequate care finds most of his needs satisfied. He is immaturely dependent, and thus secure and serene. But his serenity however satisfying, begins to cloy, and he strikes out and attains a degree of independent security with *its* attendant serenity. At the same time he is beginning to emancipate himself from his immature dependency. The two processes go on at the same time.

Chart IV shows the development of the security patterns in the early years. The first graph shows the progress of emancipation from infancy to twenty-one, the hypothetical point of completion of this process and the point of termination of immature dependent security. The gradual increase in independent security is shown by the solid line. From this graph it is apparent that the rate of emancipation is faster than the acquisition of independent security and that at sixteen the youth is especially vulnerable, for he has deserted the agent who looks after his immature years before he has acquired a high degree of independent security.

At this point another security pattern comes to the rescue, differing in a definite manner from the other two. (See second graph.) Immature dependent security means a one-way dependence; with independent security a child had learned to depend upon himself; now mature dependent security is acquired through learning how to arrange a

CHART IV

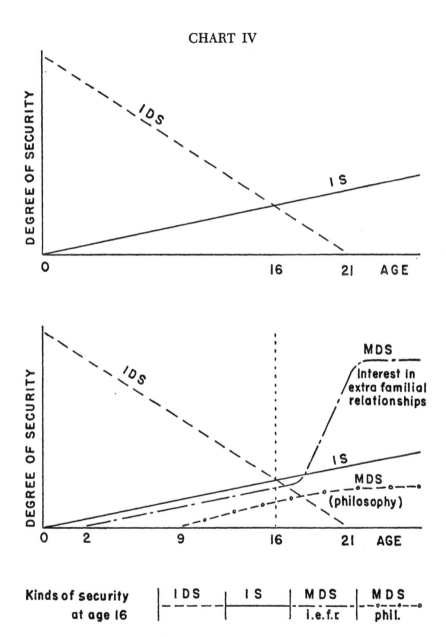

mutual dependency pattern between two persons. The interaction is reciprocal. Each one depends upon the other.

The problems of the second decade of life have erroneously been attributed to sexual maturation. Actually they are a reflection of what has previously been learned for working out reciprocal relationships with one's contemporaries. This long and complicated learning process (see graphs two and three of Chart IV), occupying much of an individual's effort from infancy to adolescence, is called *socialization*.

Two illustrative incidents will serve as a prelude to the discussion of socialization. A couple of two-year-old boys are standing looking out of the windows of a farmhouse at a herd of cows passing into a field. One of them happens to glance at his companion and see that he is holding a bright-coloured toy. He immediately reaches for it and takes it away from its "owner." Retaliation is prompt but unsuccessful. At this age, possession is ten-tenths of the law. The fortunate intervention of the poacher's mother restores the toy, but not peace. The interesting aftermath is that the child who has regained the toy returns to watch the cows, wholly uninterested in the other boy's noisy reaction.

I myself was involved in another social incident. While still director of the Institute of Child Study I was accustomed to sit in the lobby of our school on occasion and watch the young children as they were called for at the end of the day. A five-year-old girl, carrying a large picture which she had painted that day in class, showed it to the school secretary and then to me. Across the top the teacher had written a title at the child's request. After a few moments of silent appreciation I asked, pointing to the title, "What does that say?" She looked at me sympathetically and said in a conspirational whisper, "*I* can't read, either." Her mother appeared at this instant and the child ran towards her, turning to give me a wave of her hand as assurance that she would not betray me.

Similar incidents have been observed by every parent and teacher of young children. The first incident I cited pictures the beginning of the child's awareness of other human beings. The second illustrates that the social techniques learned in dealing with others may well be called "charm." There are, of course, lapses in this learning process.

The human infant is not born a social being. There is no evidence of any kind to suggest an instinctive social behaviour pattern or a felt need for human companionship at birth. All social behaviour patterns and social gratifications in human beings are learned. These statements do not apply to infra-human species. As applied to humans they are easily made and must be justified or at least defended. Recalling the guesses we made about consciousness, we can guess further that social development arises out of the conscious capacity to classify and interpret. Chart V illustrates the progression from a *non*-social (not *a*social) experience to a socially conscious one. All attempts to pierce the barrier of forgetfulness that has closed over the early years have proven unsuccessful. Whether in certain psychopathic states this presocial period may be recalled is a matter of conjecture.

Referring to Chart V, let us keep on guessing. A newborn child exposed to a host of new experiences will be frightened. He will be assured somewhat by the close contact of a comfortable crib and perhaps intrigued by the murmur of soft noises. These differences from his foetal environment pose a challenge: to distinguish between the stability and continuity of the one experience and the unstable distractability and fascination of the other, the latter more interesting, the former more assuring. At least there is a basis of differentiating and classifying. The steady background is taken for granted. The changing world is further classified into those changes that are *regular* in recurrence and hence become familiar, such as the alternation of day and night, and those which are *irregular*. Irregular changes include such events as the appearance of the agent, a visual object which precedes various experiences such as being picked up; changing position and gaining a new line of vision; a change in auditory environment (mother singing); change from discomfort (damp and cold) to a former comfortable (dry and warm) condition. He learns that some of these experiences can to some extent be controlled. By persistent effort he can grasp a toy within reach; he can change his own auditory environment by crying, squealing, or yelling, with intermittent stops. But some of the irregular experiences remain beyond his control, such as falling over when he wishes to sit up, falling down when he tries to stand, and occasional painful but apparently unavoidable episodes of falling or bumping. Control gradually improves. It is of two kinds: direct control, such as throwing or catching a ball, and indirect control, such as smiling to control his agent. After some weeks he learns that smiling can bring objects that are interesting and rewarding closer. By uttering certain sounds he learns to control objects that are even further away.

Finally he identifies the object of *direct* control (the *self*) with the unstable, irregular, *indirectly* controlled objects (other human beings). He has become social. He numbers himself among the objects he will later call "human beings." He will make the mistake of including in

CHART V

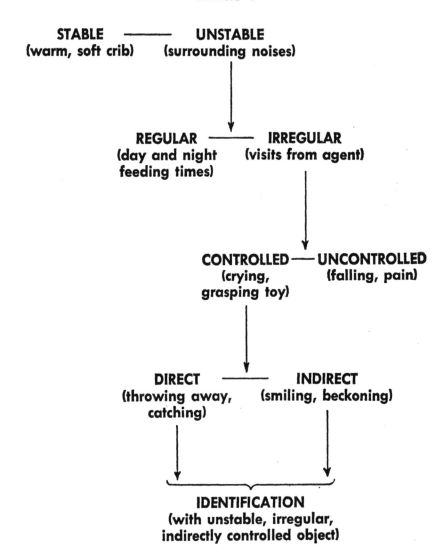

the human category other objects with seemingly similar attributes, for example pet dogs or cats, and even dolls. The distinction between animate and inanimate is made later.

As soon as his identification with others takes place he begins to appreciate what they may contribute to his needs and wants, and he begins to acquire forms of behaviour that enable him to control them. From this stage on, most if not all of his conscious life is either dominated by a social setting or has one as its background. He is never alone again. Loneliness is a heightened awareness of the companionship one lacks. To "want to be alone" is a variant of *social* behaviour.

In order to understand the universal appearance of social behaviour in human beings one must recall the basic motives that direct their development—the attitudes, appetites, and emotions. These have been fully discussed in my earlier books, *Parents and the Pre-School Child* and *Understanding the Young Child*. Consider six of these needs (Chart VI): the attitudes of like and dislike, the appetites for change and sex, and the emotions of assuagement of fear and direction of anger. These are the *only* needs that can be satisfied socially. A dinner party is undoubtedly a social gathering, but the food, though it satisfies the appetite of hunger, is merely the bait to entice companionship, so that other social gratifications may ensue. These gratifications are hopefully derived from the wit of the guests whom one likes, the challenge of the arguments, and the feeling of camaraderie. There may also be other derived wants such as prestige, social advancement, or business advantage. These latter wants evolve much beyond childhood. Often the food, except where a group of gourmets are celebrating, or a crowd of refugees are being fed, is incidental to the gathering. (Only cannibals may be said to *dine* socially.) To be sure, good food and discriminating drink, pave the way for more pleasant and perhaps more scintillating post-prandial inter-communication, but the needs that are satisfied are the appetite of change, the feeling of belonging, the excitement of competition in argument, and the possibility of being jolted by the novelty of the imagination of others.

An examination of the six needs capable of being satisfied socially will indicate that each of them may also be satisfied *non*-socially; e.g., likes and dislikes may be exercised in art and other collections; change may be found in travelling and reading; sex, in onanism; familiar elements, in one's home and possessions; competition, in the challenge of research and explorations. Thus, to reiterate, one doesn't need companions, but one may learn to want them.

We tend to choose companionship. We do not *need* others but most

CHART VI

NEEDS		WANTS
ATTITUDE Likes		Any object can serve, including an-other person
Dislikes antagonism (restriction)		Pain
		Force, including an enfolding em-brace
	INDIVIDUALLY SATISFIED	
APPETITES Change		Anything new; knowledge induces boredom
Sex		Manipulation, of self or others, con-quest, etc.
EMOTIONS Assuagement of fear		Any familiar object or trusted person
Anger competition challenge		A difficult task or an opposing person or authority
	SOCIALLY SATISFIED	

of us learn to *want* them because they can supply a better, easier, richer, more fruitful background for the conscious gratification of wants than we can supply through our own efforts in a non-social environment. But there will be some who choose to avoid or disdain human companionship as others choose to seek it.

On examining the six needs which may be satisfied socially, it is apparent that no one person can serve to satisfy all six. What persons may satisfy what needs depends largely on the state of sophistication of a society as expressed in its rules or customs. For example, in our western society a mother traditionally should be a refuge from fear but cannot be an object of sex attraction. A husband may be such an object to his wife, but must stop short of fulfilment if other needs loom large. A husband should be a refuge in time of apprehension and a wife should reciprocate in similar circumstances. A husband and wife should not be in competition except perhaps in trivial situations such as bridge (if bridge can be said to be trivial). Parents should not be *too* exciting for young children lest they verge towards objects of fear. So the nature of the society in which a child grows up, and the variety of its customs, will dictate the kind of social choices he must make. Since there is no instinctive pattern, provision should be made for him to learn as early as possible how to choose properly. As a child becomes socially minded at around two years of age, provision should be made for him to gain social experience among his peers. This is one great value of the well-planned nursery school. The social mistakes he makes in these early years, such as stealing, cheating, betrayal, violence, have trivial consequences compared to those that could ensue later on.

The social patterns which each person acquires depend upon the social goals he has set up. If one person learns to persuade another, quite subtly, to do what he wants him to do, and if in the process he arranges for the other to think he is following his own wish, then the former is said to have "charm." If, on the other hand, he learns no patterns to induce others to rally 'round, then he is said to lack charm.

Mature dependent security is attained through a person's own efforts. In order to gratify the wants which were formerly taken care of by the agents of his immaturity, he must now seek other agents farther afield. He may choose companions who will act as parental substitutes; this will only postpone his emancipation. Or he may choose a new type of companion. In this new relationship he will contribute to the security of his companion in return for a like contribution from him. Mature dependency always involves a two-way interaction. The proportion which each friend contributes will vary depending on which of the wants each wishes to gratify. A close, mutual, equally contributing fellowship is highly rewarding, but rare. In most cases the contribution is not truly balanced.

In each society there are, however, certain characteristics which are socially significant. Some are a part of the physical heritage of a person. In our western society, in childhood, curly blonde hair, a dimpled smile, and a graceful carriage are advantages if employed skilfully. Later on, height, bodily curves, tone of voice, graceful movement, and other accepted attributes may supplement acquired social skills. But these are immature agents because they may disappear with increasing age or go out of style. The patterns which one acquires out of a keen desire to belong and contribute grow more effective with increasing age and never go out of style.

What is true of two friends also pertains to group participation. The degree of intimacy or interdependence depends on the extent of the contribution made by each member of the group, and the amount of gratification each member derives from belonging. Thus a small group which for some time has gone hunting together for a fortnight every year derives a deep feeling of belonging because each one contributes a great deal to sustaining the group intact. A group of neighbours organized to present a petition to the city council hardly survives as a group, since its only mutual memory is of the petition.

The Ideal Mature Dependent Relationship

Persons seeking mature dependent security ideally have to acquire the skills by which a pattern of mutual interdependence is created. A mutually interdependent relationship in its ideal form may be described as follows: each individual will see certain physical qualities in the other which appeal and which will not decrease in their appeal because of change in fashion. He will also appreciate mannerisms, ideas, principles, and ideals in the other, and this appreciation will survive more critical and detailed familiarity over the years. Conversely, each will not see in the other qualities that offend and irritate him.

Neither will assume the right of ascendancy over the other, except where one, through training and experience, has acquired a status which the other does not possess to the same degree (for example, one may be a concert pianist, the other an amateur performer). Neither will feel the right to control the other except through discussion and ultimate agreement and, if necessary, compromise. This mechanism requires a skill in communication that grows only with practice as a measure of understanding is gradually achieved. Who is the boss in a mature dependent relationship is a meaningless question.

One learns that to be interesting one must be interested (how few good listeners there are!), and so each partner in a dependent relationship will acquire both common and individual skills, the former to act as a means of ensuring co-operative companionship and the latter to enhance the excitement of sharing separate experiences. In this fashion the companionship grows in its rewards and can never become boring.

A high degree of trust is developed between two people only over time. Trust is based mainly on familiarity. One gradually learns to expose to the other one's own thoughts, fears, hopes, ambitions, failures, and triumphs. It is probably impossible for one person ever to expose himself completely to another, even to a psychoanalyst or a confessor. The degree of the exposure determines the depth of the intimacy. If confidences are received and treated with attention, commendation if deserved, reasonable criticism if asked for, sympathy, affectionate humour, sound advice, or just understanding silence, and if this reception is reciprocated, then there will be no place for jealousy, envy, over-possessiveness, deception, or suspicion. Here again communication is essential, and there must be some formal as well as informal arrangements for opportunities to communicate.

Competition between two such friends is a complicated arrangement. If they are to be familiar with each other, each will learn to anticipate the moves of the other, whether in bridge, in conversational gambits, or in other areas. Providing the final outcome of competition in these relatively unimportant areas is of slight moment, the excitement is enjoyable; but competition should stop short of serious contests that may leave scars. There are so many challenges which may be met and attacked together, that there need be no room for undignified jockeying for pre-eminence.

A glance back at this short summary of an ideal mature dependent relationship will suggest several comments. What a comfortable, gratifying, enjoyable, and at times exciting companionship such an arrangement would be! In the course of *one* life how many such companions does one acquire? One if one is industrious and persistent. Two if lucky. Three?—take another careful look! But if through effort and opportunity one does acquire such a "friend" who is of the opposite sex, and marriage ensues, then the basis of this union is unusually sound.

One further need must now be added to our discussion, namely sex. The physical or physiological satisfactions in this area need not be discussed here. The modern press, theatre, radio, and TV have disclosed most if not all of the simple as well as esoteric formulae. Nor need we at this juncture discuss the aberrant patterns that seem so much in the fore in the above media.

To complete the description of the ideal mature companionship: if the two, man and woman, approximate to a high degree the above description of a friendship, then they are bound to include their heterosexual drives in the relationship. But sex in a mature dependent relationship offers much more than the sensory and sensual satisfaction of successful climacteric. Included in this experience are the intimacies of other areas, the accumulation of apparently trivial episodes of affection, simple humorous contents, shared secrets, memories relived, experimental exploration, consideration, and tenderness. These experiences and many more are products of the impact of all of the foregoing lessons that were learned, largely without a sex component but brought to bear on one of the more intimate of human physiological experiences. Sex cannot compare in depth to the serenity of intimacy of the embrace of a father and mother after the birth of a wanted child. When a husband or wife has been what is euphemistically called "unfaithful," largely because of some deficiency in meeting the foregoing description of the ideal friendship, it is usually through the pull of these apparently extraneous factors that the marriage union may continue, sometimes strengthened by the reconciliation and the implication of "fault" on both sides.

In summary we may say: to compensate for the gradual reduction of immature dependent security and the slow growth in independence, there is available a mature type of dependency for all except those whose mental capacity never exceeds a two-year level and in whom mature or independent security hardly appears. Mature dependence may be acquired through the imperative necessity to become a social being. The agent in this case is a partner, and a reciprocal relationship prevails in which each partner contributes to the security of the other.

Authority

In the welter of the earliest experiences of a child, besides those that are pleasant and relaxing, such as feeding, and those that are fascinating and exciting, such as change, among the outstanding ones there will be the repeated incidents of interruption and interference with his stream of consciousness in incidents such as dressing, changing, and washing, to which he will respond with an antagonistic reaction or at least a rebellious feeling. Gradually these episodes will crystallize in his mind into specific acts by which he is denied his goal, as when a dangerous but fascinating object is taken from his grasp. Later he will see that this process of control is exercised by a social agent, either directly through its greater strength (force) or, as the discrepancy in relative strength decreases, indirectly through persuasion, custom, guile, the "gloved fist," and other devices.

As the child begins to control his own efforts to reach his goals, he appreciates the art of bargaining. "If you don't hit me, I won't hit you." This is the period dominated by the *lex talionis*, "an eye for an eye . . ." in the jungle environment of infancy. A refinement of this in civilized groups is called "compromise" without which peace would be impossible. Self-control is not the final step towards mature dependence in this area, however.

Up to this point control has been dictated by self-interest, the privileges or gratifications derived from belonging to a group. Liberty, rights, obligations, privileges, non-aggression, law and order are the terms that will be learned and applied to the personal concepts which each individual will acquire through his own experience. One person's concept of "rights" does not necessarily coincide with that of another. Each one is seeking the greatest amount of self-interest consistent with society's customs, laws, and degree of permissiveness. A person is willing to accept the consequences of his actions provided he deems the consequences reasonable, but as soon as he considers the consequences unreasonable he will refuse to "obey." For example the liquor laws in various countries were of little effect when they were considered unreasonable. One of the world's leading scientists condoned the breaking of a law if it interfered with what he considered an infringement of personal liberty. An eminent philosopher suggests that "enlightened" self-interest is the best gauge of acceptable behaviour.

Individual preferences or communal consensuses do not seem to be rational or effective measures of an ultimate goal for a mature person, however appealing they appear. Some higher goal or value is continually sought. What it is to be is difficult to clarify. The youth in early adolescence is confused by adult inconsistency in the search for value. He will have undergone one of several training programmes. The most frequently encountered are the following:

1. He will have been inducted at an early age into one of the orthodox (conformist) faiths. He will have accepted the dogmas, disciplines, and patterns as substitute immature agents. Up to adolescence

his faith will remain strong because he will not yet have been exposed to any crisis of doubt.

2. He will have been indoctrinated against all dogma and will accept the role of an "atheist" with the same assurance, strength, and conviction as if he belonged to group 1. This is also an immature dependent security pattern.

3. He will not have been exposed except casually and coincidentally to any "religious" experience or formal training. (Children in this category are becoming more and more in evidence.)

Regardless of which of these three programmes has been followed, a dangerous period of indecision and confusion, that is, of insecurity and anxiety, strikes all young people. They all feel the need of an agent to compensate for the emancipation that has been proceeding and for the small amount of independent security that they have acquired. This is the period of the inconclusive arguments that last into the early mornings. Each generation has its own terms to describe them. In my day they were called bull-sessions. The subject of these discussions is much more often about morals and their origin than about sexual immorality and its consequences.

The outcome of these informal seminars depends on several factors, the most important of which is whether one has actually understood what is meant by the question, *Why?* Here is a simple test. An astronomer can answer with only a slight error a question on the movement of the heavenly bodies. He can pinpoint the position of any one, at any time in the future, within narrow limits. But if he were asked, "Why will that event take place?" could he answer as an astronomer? Or if a physicist is asked, "What is the rate of radio-active decay in this element?" he can answer with some assurance. But as a physicist, can he answer why? And furthermore, if each of these scientists does answer why, can the answers be subject to the same treatment as the answers to other questions in order to find out their "truth"?

Once a person appreciates the difference between the question of *why* and other questions, and the necessary difference in the answers, he must find these answers or remain insecure. He probably will frame the second, *why*, question as, "What is the purpose of life?" It may be conjectured what effect the resultant analysis has on the resolution of insecurity for a person in each of the three groups we have described.

A member of group one whose emancipation from his immature agent has been prolonged may be unaffected by the discussion, accepting the orthodox faith of his forebears as a matter of course and with increased assurance. Or the discussion may disturb his faith for the moment or for a longer period, in which case he may join the other groups, or change his allegiance to another orthodoxy (conversion or apostasy, depending upon which side is speaking), or he may regain his faith in stronger form. If a crisis has previously disturbed his faith, the discussions may arouse doubt, which is the symptom of insecurity. Doubt may be resolved as above, or the individual may be thrust into a period of severe confusion and despair.

A member of group two, if he seriously appreciates the implications of the "why" question, will never be the same again. A denial of purpose, once it is appreciated, can only lead to futility, and so he must either reinforce his own rationale for believing what he formerly held as true and unassailable or join group three.

A member of group three will already have experienced some episodes of insecurity. He may have tried the answers of groups one and two and found them wanting. He is, however, ready to appreciate fully the necessity to answer the question, "What is the purpose of life?" if he is to have "peace of mind," that is, serenity.

He looks for a mature agent upon whom he can depend and in whom he can place his trust. In return he is willing to accept the consequences of embracing a code of ethics which demands a rigid control of the unilateral gratification of wants and satisfaction of needs. There can be no compromise with one's conscience.

The mature agent in human interrelationships has been described as another human being. A relationship of mutual interdependence, varying from close intimacy to mere acquaintance, requires that each person, acting as agent for the other, must contribute towards the maintenance of the relationship. The feeling of serenity which accompanies this mature dependent security also varies in its satisfaction from the depth and warmth of feeling in the possession of a close friend to the tenuous feeling of belonging to a large group, such as a nation.

However the mature agent sought by a member of group three is not a personalized deity. Human traits are in themselves not fitting nor sufficient. It is more important to understand the reasons for things. The more intellectually trained one is the more one experiences awe, wonder, and amazement upon observing the functioning of the universe. How little is known! How much may be unknowable! How little is man! The hero-worship of pre-puberty is sloughed off, to be supplanted by the urgent necessity to accept a code of ethics derived in some way, certainly not by human reasoning, to fill in the gap between human achievement and human inadequacy.

The code becomes the human core of one's belief in the transcendental. The contribution which the individual makes is the acceptance of the consequences of following the code. Any transgression or violation is not an offence against a personal deity to be wiped out by some form of conciliation but, far more significant in a mature person, an appreciation of one's own inadequacy—one has made a human mistake. This appreciation is the origin of a conscience, from the accusation of which one cannot escape.

In this fashion one pays no tribute; one was never exacted. Rather, in the attempt to acquire various qualities of personality such as mercy, consideration, pity, loyalty, charity, and above all tolerance, one achieves the supreme accomplishment of man—human dignity.

9 · Deputy Agents

In which it is shown that deputy agents—postponement, re-interpretation, redirection, and denial—arise out of healthy attempts to solve problems, and become hazardous only in their extreme and solidified forms.

WHEN AN INDIVIDUAL is trying to deal with a situation, he may face up to it, make a decision, use his "know-how," and accept the consequence. If he does, he is using his independent security. However, his efforts may take him into false channels which do not lead to a real solution but by which he avoids the real consequence at least temporarily. These false channels are called "deputy agents." Deputy agents are devices an individual uses to carry him over a period of insecurity until he is willing to accept the consequences of a genuine decision. They work by freeing him of his insecurity at least temporarily, but they lead to no adequate permanent solution. And so, on being asked, "Who took the fresh cake from the cupboard?" the young boy, wishing to escape rebuke or punishment, answers, "Not me." This avoids the consequence for the moment. But it has real hazards: first it may be discovered that he did take it and a worse consequence follows such as being forbidden cake for a week and also being designated a "liar." The epithet means nothing to him, but apparently it has great and dreadful significance to his parents. Second, if he is older, even though he is not found out, he finds he has done something that goes against his code. He has offended his mature dependent agent. This results in even greater insecurity; he worries or castigates himself so he confesses, thus attempting to restore his dependent security.

All children in the process of learning use these false solutions.

Whether they should be called deputy agents at this stage is a moot point. In attempting to reach their goals, children try various means that they think will be effective, they lie, steal, blame, day-dream, hide, boast. In nursery-school children, I have found that two or three of these techniques are used every day, but they are frequently varied and altered. Ten-year-olds use a lesser variety, but the ones they do use they employ more frequently. They retain the ones which they have found work best. Of course, no child is born with deputy agents; they are learned, and it could be demonstrated that in societies which place the most restrictions on people, the greater number of deputy agents are used.

There are four deputy areas to be described here. The description will be in everyday terms, not in the jargon of pathology. What we will describe are sensible methods of dealing with situations, but methods which if exaggerated, used inappropriately, or relied on continually, become automatic and in due course become hazardous to mental health.

This is a new approach, for it assumes that abnormal behaviour is not inherently different from normal behaviour. All people in growing up use methods for dealing with insecurity which are designed to avoid accepting consequences. Many are dropped, but some remain in a permanent exaggerated form and the person who depends on them forgets the nature of the device he is using. It is at this stage that he loses insight, and its loss is rightly considered malignant or abnormal. An individual who has insight knows when he is using a deputy and is willing to accept it or seek an alternative solution later.

Postponement, Reinterpretation, Redirection, and Denial

As Chart VII shows, postponement, reinterpretation, redirection, and denial may all be used as sound means towards achieving independent security. They become increasingly dangerous as deputy agents as the frequency of their use rises towards a permanent or pathological state. This final state always involves complete lack of insight.

POSTPONEMENT

A decision to postpone is an interim decision made in lieu of a final one. A person may postpone his final decision because he feels that it is necessary to gather more information or because he has an immediate commitment and has not time to consider his decision properly and still fulfil that commitment. He feels that by waiting he

CHART VII

A. METHODS OF DEALING WITH INSECURITY

B. RESULTS OF INDEPENDENTLY SECURE USE OF METHODS IN (A)

C. DEPUTY AGENT SECURITY, RESULTING FROM COMPLETE DEPENDENCE ON METHODS IN (A) AND USE OF FOLLOWING TECHNIQUES IN ORDER OF INCREASING DANGER

tension, chronic worry

A	B	C (in order of increasing danger →)
I. POSTPONEMENT	judgment caution wisdom relaxation	tendency to put off till tomorrow → procrastination → indecision → suggestibility → credulity → lack of will
II. REINTERPRETATION (RATIONALIZATION)	reason imagination fantasy invention creativity humour identification	tendency to daydream → explanation in terms of "sour grapes" → hero worship → hallucination → delusions of grandeur
III. REDIRECTION (ASSIGNMENT OF BLAME)	conscience acceptance of authority acceptance of responsibility empathy	tendency to pass the buck → intolerance → blame → suspicion → prejudice → accusation
IV. DENIAL	sense of proportion	exaggeration of trivia → minimizing of responsibility → repression → hypochondria—psychosomatic ailments → obsession—compulsion → shyness → fainting → amnesia

will be better able to make a more sensible decision and thereby effect better consequences. This postponement of a decision leads to the development of judgment. Instead of being foolhardy or precipitous, the individual is willing to accept the fact that the insecurity will continue. He may put off dealing with his business letters until Monday, but he knows there is nothing requiring immediate action. He is not anxious. To do one thing always means to let another wait. This is called organization and planning. However, planning carried too far into a rigid routine grows into compulsiveness and becomes dangerous, for anxiety is aroused if the organized plan breaks at any point.

From the astute use of postponement the personality trait develops of being cautious without being timid. This may be called wisdom; it is the result of the accumulation of a great deal of experience in dealing with insecure situations. Wisdom is the sign of maturity. It cannot be gathered from a textbook or in a short time. A young person cannot have wisdom in this sense; he has not had time to practice it. Child geniuses can learn skills such as music or art as they concentrate on them. But there is no way of concentrating on the skill required for making decisions in everyday life. There is no method by which one can learn how to deal with another person, except by living through experiences with other people.

If postponement is used as a device for avoiding consequences without providing for a later decision, it becomes a deputy agent. "Putting off until tomorrow what you should do today" becomes putting off *indefinitely* what you should do now. Such behaviour is called procrastination, a deliberate attempt to avoid making a decision and thereby avoid its consequences. As the habit spreads a person becomes indecisive and, since anxiety remains until a decision is made, he becomes a worrier. Worry is anxiety which one does not want to accept. Worry increases tension. This anxious state in ordinary parlance is called "lack of will power." With it goes increased credulity and suggestibility. Whether the device of postponement is dangerous depends on whether or not a person has set a time at which he is going to deal with the matter and whether he actually does so. If he continues simply to put it off, the problem grows, and he has what is called "an anxiety neurosis."

It is often difficult to decide the point at which a constructive pattern changes into a vulnerable one. For example, as one becomes more skilled in learning to accept insecurity, one can relax even though one has decided to postpone a decision, and this relaxing under anxiety is one of the most difficult patterns to learn. However, there is a point at which certain people relax so much that they make no subsequent decision to expend any effort. This is certainly pathological. On the other hand, relaxation may turn into what is called "laziness"—a moral judgment by one person of another person's behaviour.

REINTERPRETATION

Reinterpreting the insecure position involves the perception of a variety of ways in which the problem might be dealt with. One form of reinterpretation is *reasoning*. Reasoning is deciding on the method by which to deal with insecurity. The willingness to accept the challenge of trying something new is called imagination. Reasoning precedes imagination in a child. No child is born with imagination. It develops from children's attempts to reinterpret situations so as to solve new problems. They use primitive logic which is based on a belief that what has happened before will happen again. As children become willing to accept the challenge of anxiety, imagination evolves. Some people grow up without any imagination, others are willing to explore the limits of possibility. This latter course leads to fantasy and invention, traits which all parents would like to see in their children and which every university president extols at opening ceremonies: "We want people who refuse to be conformists, but will go out in new ways into unexplored areas!" Unfortunately those who do so frequently come under threat of expulsion.

If reasoning and imagination do not enable the individual to put out independent effort to deal with a situation, they turn into the deputy agents of day-dreams. Day-dreams under control are a form of imagination, and humour arises out of one's skill in altering a situation to make it more acceptable without denying that it exists or attempting to avoid dealing with it. However, day-dreams may turn into a fantasy of lies by which the reality of the situation is obliterated. The individual becomes less mentally healthy.

Another aspect of reinterpretation is argument. When an individual argues he is attempting to alter the situation according to his bias at the moment. All arguments are employed in order to alter the problem; not to fit the facts, but to fit what the individual would like the facts to be. This is called rationalization, and as a child increases his skill in rationalizing he uses the technique to make excuses for not having done what he knows he should have done.

What is known as the "sour grapes" attitude is a distortion of the facts as the individual knows them in an attempt to make them more conducive to the decision that has already been made. For example a child who wants an ice cream cone is refused it. So he says, "I don't want it anyhow. It's only old strawberry."

Later on when reinterpretation has been used again and again, it becomes exaggerated and emerges as a delusion or a hallucination. A person actually makes his perceptions and beliefs as he wants them to be. They are no longer based on reality. He has lost insight and has instead an effective device at hand for avoiding the anxiety of an insecure position by having his distortions already made. How difficult it is to recognize the thin line between the constructive use of day-dreams, imagination, and humour and their destructive use in fantasies that make effort unnecessary. To most people the image of a soufflé is hardly as satisfying as eating a real one. But if one becomes perfectly satisfied with merely thinking about one, he has developed hallucinations. He accepts the imagery as reality. Such is the end result of reinterpretation.

REDIRECTION

A person redirects his insecurity when he attributes it to a different source. He blames someone or something else. If he feels the problem is due to someone else, then he does not have to accept the consequences of making a decision about it. It is taken out of his realm and placed elsewhere.

Redirection can be benign. In an analysis of a situation by redirection one begins to discover one's own contribution to it. Here is the origin of the emergence of conscience. One accepts the blame; one realizes one's insecurity has been brought about by one's own failures or omissions. This leads towards an acceptance of a code of personal responsibility.

A great deal of redirection arises from the necessity of living in a world in which there are various authorities. In the early years parental authority must be lived and dealt with. It becomes the original model for all authorities to be encountered later. It is interesting to ask how the child does learn to live with it. For to his amazement, authority is usually interfering with what he wants to do. In order to accept this interference a child learns how to avoid the consequence of coming into contact with it. He learns to blame something else such as the cat, or someone else, such as his brother or sister, teacher or companion. The embodiment of authority is, of course, the mother and father, but at the same time they are his agents of immature dependence. Their object in exercising authority is to train him to accept consequences, and to eliminate themselves as the agents of discipline. They are interested in the development of self-discipline. When self-discipline is achieved the child makes his own rules and lives by them. They serve as the basis, not only for the behaviour pattern which he will employ, but also for the development of a conscience. A conscience—which must be acquired—may be described as the feeling a person has when he has failed to meet the requirements of his own rules and regulations.

All children must grow up under some authority if they are to survive, but the kinds of authority and the atmospheres of authority in which children grow and develop are manifold. There are authorities which are severe, cruel, kindly, indifferent, possessive, reasonable, systematic, slip-shod, and so on. The child will respond and react to whatever kind of authority is manifested. As inconsistency in authority is almost universal, the child will develop some kind of a deputy agent in order to avoid the consequences of the kind of discipline or authority under which he must live. And the most common use of the deputy agent of redirection is to avoid the consequences of unjust authority by attempting to place the onus of the infringement of the rules upon someone or something else. In the early years, when a child avoids consequences by attempting to blame someone who is in authority, he has a feeling that he has placed the onus unfairly on someone else and feels guilty about so doing. His feeling of guilt may carry over in the future to other situations in which he is dealing with authority. As it becomes more widely used, it arouses a spirit of intolerance, because in order to justify one's blaming someone else, one must develop a feeling of resentment towards him. This is the basis of prejudices. Such resentments may consolidate and become obsessions. In these, not only is there resentment against such a person or a thing, but in the presence or even at the thought of such persons or things resentment inevitably manifests itself.

The final stage of the deputy agent of redirection is that in which one develops feelings of persecution. Then one feels that the whole world is against one, both in general and in specific instances. For example, one feels that there are agencies at work to curtail one's freedom of activity, and one thus finds ample justification to retaliate against such persecutory agencies. In this last stage, of course, the individual has lost insight. A very serious kind of mental illness develops which by its very nature makes any kind of treatment more or less ineffective.

DENIAL

The fourth category of deputy agents is that of denial. It occurs when the individual maintains that there is no problem, or that there is no necessity to decide. He attempts to evade the consequences of behaviour by believing that there is nothing to consider.

To the infant all problems have exactly the same urgency. They consist of one thing: he wants, he can't get, and then he raises hell. This is the common procedure in all infants. As one grows up, one learns to differentiate between the trivial, the average, and the urgent, and the development of this sense of proportion is a sign of maturity. One learns not to make mountains out of molehills and, equally important, not to make molehills out of mountains. Some people never learn to differentiate between the trivia and the important, and spend as much energy on dealing with what tie to wear as what woman to marry. How does one develop a proper sense of proportion? Time is required, and there is a marked change as one becomes more mature. A sense of proportion has to be learned and becomes a differentiating aspect of personality. If as a child grows up he learns that certain things are more important than others, he acquires the ability of saying to himself, "This situation requires some degree of thinking," before he makes a decision.

A child may be presented with a situation where he must make an immediate decision without an opportunity of acquiring all of the facts. For example, he may find himself with a group of three or four of his companions on the bank of a strange stream and one of them suggests that they jump in and swim. He feels that although he can swim quite well it isn't a wise thing to jump into a strange place, and so he decides that he will not go in. He must stand up against the judgment of his peers and accept the consequences of being called a "chicken." The ability to know when one is incapacitated, unskilled, ignorant, or unwilling to accept the consequences that might be dangerous, is called moral courage. Moral courage is a function of learning how to deal with insecurity by being able to recognize it and to reject or avoid the consequences that might arise if one precipitated a decision. But at the same time this means that one must accept the consequences of retreating in another direction from the necessity of making a decision.

Development of the deputy agent of denial starts very early. For example, when a child shows fear, and the parent is suggesting to the child (who knows that he *is* afraid) that his fear does not exist, the fear is denied. However, all fears are real to the person who experiences them. One should not suggest that there is nothing to be afraid of, but rather imply, "Go ahead and be afraid. By being so you don't lose anything in my estimation." Later one discusses the fear to see what it is all about and how it can be dealt with. In this way one trains a child not to deny that there is an insecurity, but rather that there is a technique for dealing with it.

There are two forms of denial by which a person with apparent legitimacy avoids an issue. One is by being *ill* and the other is by *forgetting*. Having postponed a decision temporarily by being ill, or permanently by the ruse of forgetting it entirely, one appears to have dealt with the situation. Forgetting and illness lead into two kinds of vulnerable methods of dealing with insecure situations in the category of denial. If illness has made it possible to avoid consequences—if, for example one is ill in the morning and is excused from going to school, and hence does not have to write examinations—then illness becomes a very facile device to use. Later on these illnesses, not feigned, but rather induced through the necessity of finding a method of avoidance, lead to all of the intricacies of psychosomatic medicine, of which migraine headaches, perhaps, are the most common and the most advertised. Eventually the more permanent state may develop in which one has an illness of such a nature that one isn't expected to accept any consequences. This is called hypochondria. Such illness is an easy technique for avoiding having to make any decisions at all.

Forgetting, of course may be trivial. One forgets to keep an appointment which one wanted to avoid, or to perform a task, relay a message, post a letter, buy certain shopping items. This form of behaviour leads to a more serious and permanent state which is called amnesia. Though not as common as one would be led to believe from fiction and the movies, amnesia nevertheless occurs frequently enough. It becomes a very effective method of avoiding the consequences of having to deal with a situation, for in amnesia the situation itself has been fully and successfully denied.

We have now described the four categories of deputy agents, and in a brief review, we must recall that in infants, regression is a very common method of dealing with insecure situations. Regressive formulae are by all means the most common form of avoidance in children. Gradually children acquire deputy agents. It would be a mistake perhaps to call these deputies mature devices, but nevertheless they are the same ones that appear later on in adult patterns of behaviour. We have suggested that in early life children manifest all kinds of deputy agents, but as they grow up only those that are successful become fixed, and it is these fixed deputy agents that provide the esccentricities and individual patterns which make for the personality of an adult individual. To some extent they give the person "character." With some nostalgia one recalls that a friend, "never went to wash his hands till dinner was on the table," or "he could make a good story out of the most appalling situations," or "she always forgot to put on the salt." A person may be characterized by his use of deputies and accepted perhaps for them rather than in spite of them. Whether they are solidified to the point where they are disabling is largely a matter of circumstances. Success and failure in dealing with life's urgencies are the most important influencing factors.

If one is able to maintain insight and if one from time to time reviews one's deputy agents and decides to make appropriate decisions when they should be made, then it is possible to carry on without any disabling crisis. The disabling patterns do not suddenly emerge but are derived from those deputy agents which have been found successful. The pattern of an individual's breakdown can be predicted from a thorough knowledge of his deputy agents. These devices become exaggerated through the lack of insight. Recreating insight is what psychotherapy is supposed to do. Recognition of the deputy agent is not enough. One has to learn to deal with patterns of insecurity in such a way that consequences are not avoided.

10 · Decisions

In which it is shown that making decisions is a continuous process; that the variables involved are complex; that making decisions is easier than accepting the consequences; that the success of a decision can only be viewed in terms of one's final goal. In which the uses of authority are examined and the techniques studied for making choices turn out right.

RECENTLY an elderly and outwardly successful business executive said half jestingly that the hardest decision he had to make was "to get out of bed every morning," and then he added half seriously, "I suppose when I retire I will have the same difficulty deciding to sleep in!"

There is a universal misapprehension that decisions are relatively rare in everyday life, that they occur only on fairly momentous occasions and are turning points in a person's career. As a matter of fact, as we saw earlier, since man is a conscious organism, he constantly selects from among alternatives. Selection is a continuous aspect of consciousness which in its facility for attending, chooses from the many impacts of its total surroundings. The content of one's surroundings changes regularly and quite rapidly, whether one is idly watching the changing flicker in an open fire, reading the pages of a book, or working on a problem of mathematics.

The peculiar quality of *deciding* is the association of selection with action. Action follows the selection of the goal towards which one is striving at any moment. The placing of one foot in front of the other when walking produces a series of decisive actions. In adulthood these have become more or less automatic through repetition, but at one time a young child learning to walk is highly conscious of his selection of specific actions. One's childhood experience is partly recalled when one recovers from a stumble, or arises after a prolonged stay in bed during an illness.

At the next opportunity, try standing aside to watch the line slowly proceeding past the counters in a self-service restaurant. One person will hesitate, put something back, then select quickly, pushed by the line, and look longingly at the first selection, another will pass along taking one dish here, another there, with little hesitation or *apparent* decision. There are many patterns of deciding, but there is a general plan into which they all fit. The following conscious steps, with some overlapping, may be identified in all acts of decision: (1) motive, (2) goal or incentive, (3) preparation for decision, (4) decision, (5) action, (6) consequences of action, (7) dealing with consequences.

In many instances some of these steps seem to have been eliminated, but a close analysis shows that in every case each of these steps have been included. For example, the man in the restaurant who passed through quickly (1) was hungry, (2) wanted a salad, (3) judged that there were no alternatives of equal value, (4) decided, (5) took a salad, (6) ate it, (7) enjoyed it as he anticipated. Aside from steps 6 and 7 which occupied some time, the other steps had been foreshortened by repetition and also by habit acquired by this subject in this milieu.

Variables of Decision-Making

At the Canadian Psychological Association Conference in 1958, I described the complexity of the variables involved in decision-making. The remainder of this section is from an abstract of that address printed in the *Canadian Journal of Psychology*, vol. 12, no. 3 (1958), and used with the permission of the editors.

Chart VIII suggests that at least ten variables are involved, to varying degrees, in any decision-making episode and, since every moment of consciousness' is a decision-making episode, it can easily be seen how complicated a theory of human behaviour must be, whatever its starting point.

The ten variables in Chart VIII are not necessarily in order of importance. Each of them, as the diagram suggests, represents a possible continuum, for which a three, five, or seven point scale might be constructed. These scales would be about as reliable as such scales usually are. A brief description of each variable will illustrate how an introspective technique yields information.

(1) Decisions are obviously urgent or trivial, depending largely upon a value judgment by the individual concerned. An urgent decision

CHART VIII

VARIABLES IN DECISION-MAKING

DECISIONS

GOAL

1. Urgent	⟵———————————⟶	**Trivial**
2. Irretrievable	⟵———————————⟶	**Recoverable**
3. Automatized	⟵———————————⟶	**Unique**

Ethics

4. Acceptable (conformity)	⟵———————⟶	**Unacceptable** (non-conformity)

Anxiety

5. Fascination	⟵———————————⟶	**Repugnance**

Motivation

6. Basic	⟵———————————⟶	**Acquired**
Like (preference)	⟵———————⟶	**Dislike**
Dominance (social)	⟵———————⟶	**Submission**

CONSEQUENCES

CAUSALITY

7. Determinate	⟵———————————⟶	**Capricious**

Knowledge

8. Certainty	⟵———————————⟶	**Doubt**

Acceptance

9. Independent	⟵———————————⟶	**Dependent**

Time

10. Immediate	⟵———————————⟶	**Ultimate**

BEFORE

AFTER

Causal process

might be the buying of one house or another; a trivial one, whether to put the left or right sock on first.

(2) In a literal sense, no decision can ever be made again. Once made, it becomes part of one's past. But there are decisions which *appear* to be recoverable or revokable, as by exchanging goods at a store, or divorcing after marriage; and others which are clearly irretrievable, such as jumping into space from a plane.

(3) Some decisions have become automatized, such as turning the door knob to enter a room; others are unique, such as the first decision made by a novice in a profession, presented with his first case.

(4) In the area of ethical judgment, the field is wide open. It is unlikely that an individual's attitude towards his fellow-man or his code of ethics is ever absent, however negligible it may appear at times. It may appear dubious that one can place ethics on a seven-point scale—but after all there are venial as well as mortal sins.

(5) One attribute of decision-making is the inevitable feeling of anxiety. It is a mistake, however, to think that anxiety is always unpleasant. To some people indecision can be an exceedingly pleasant experience, as witness the shopping practices of well-to-do consumers, and the tension occasioned by dangerous situations in sport. Gambling, too, is prominent in human behaviour. Of course, there are times when having to make a decision is most unpleasant. Whether decision-making is pleasant or unpleasant for an individual may be a matter of training.

(6) The relative importance of basic as opposed to acquired motives is a subject for long inquiry. Two continua have been indicated. (It is interesting that, in the mathematical models proposed in the economic literature, the suggestion is made that indifference may be measured on a continuum. This kind of psychological paradox vitiates much of the significance of the mathematical formulae.) The other continuum is in the area of dominance and submission, two acquired aspects of social behaviour which are difficult to measure, but which are inevitable concomitants of decision-making.

The second main division of the attributes of decision-making is in the field of consequences, which occur, of course, after decision has been made. Once a decision has been made, however, the consequences of that decision are involved in the making of the next one; thus, although the consequences of a decision come later, nevertheless the accumulated experience of consequences is part of the apperceptive mass of the decision-making.

(7) Whether the concept of causality is ever expressed in detail

or seen clearly as a thesis, an individual always stands somewhere on a teeter-totter, balancing between a concept of the universe that is deterministic and one that is wholly capricious. It is obvious that the decision made at any given time is a function of the individual's position at that time on this scale. Hence the irritated complaint of the mathematician that individuals are not consistent.

(8) With the growth of experience it should be possible to refine and improve one's judgment by reference to the accuracy of one's predictions of the consequences of previous decisions. Whether one's knowledge is adequate or accurate depends on experience and the use of authorities, but this is not nearly as significant an aspect of decision-making as the next variable, namely, acceptance.

(9) The acceptance or attempted rejection of consequences becomes a highly significant aspect of decision-making very early in life, and it is in this area that the impact of decision-making on personality is most apparent.

(10) The more immediate the consequences of an act as envisaged by a decider, the more likely he is to refine his judgment and learn, either to accept the consequences or to modify his decision. Some consequences, however, are projected far into the future—indeed, into infinity, as with eternal punishment. This tends to impede learning. One reason for a student's failure at university, for example, may be his inability to project the consequences of his present behaviour to a point even four years hence.

Whether or not these ten variables exhaust decision-making is a matter for research. The challenge that we hand to the mathematician is to take these ten variables, arrange the continua so that the intervals are equal, and then construct a model, which will predict what an individual (not a *group*) will do (not *may* do) in a specific situation. After all, the physicist had only three variables—energy, mass, and velocity!

Successful Decisions

It is far easier to obtain at least what has the reputable appearance of being a measure of decision-making, than to establish the degree to which an individual is accepting the consequences. One's ability to make decisions is a reflection of one's efficiency and skill. But one's willingness to accept the consequence is far more important in terms of one's state of mental health.

Current studies of decision-making, using machines and other gadgets, are intriguing, but cover only a very limited aspect of the whole matter. They usually measure the time it takes to make a decision—such as which of two buttons to push to make a light go on or to get a candy. The light or candy is the reward (now called positive reinforcement) and the non-light or non-candy the punishment (now called negative reinforcement). All of which takes us back to our long-enunciated theory of consequences. As the effect of practice is brought in to establish the choice of the right light, it gets involved with a theory of learning, which is another story.

These studies may eventually lead somewhere. (I hope so, as several of my staff are interested in them.) But they leave out the crux of the whole matter, namely, that of motive and goal.

The individual decides in terms of what *he* wants, that is, what self-established rather than outer-imposed goal he wants to reach. Making a light go on or getting a candy may be a deep want for some subjects, and of no significance at all for others. For example, Billy may dislike candy intensely, Johnny already may have had a surfeit of it, and Danny is, perhaps, a candy addict. To assume that an adult-established goal has the same importance for all children is to miss the essential point of decision-making. An individual decides in terms of *his* goal, and his reward or punishment (reinforcement) is his evaluation of his success or failure, that is, whether he thinks his decision takes him closer to, or further away from attaining his wants. He finds the goal has receded or come closer as a result of his decision.

This can be demonstrated easily in both educational and clinical work. A child in school is not learning his lessons (teacher's goal); he is making a nuisance of himself, disturbing the class, having his *confrères* all laugh at his antics. The teacher punishes him for this, i.e., she makes him stand in the corridor or sends him to the principal. Eventually he may be expelled. But in terms of *his* goal—to gain notoriety among his classmates, or not have to go to school at all— each episode has been a success, and eventually, of course, through his own series of decisions, he obtains exactly what he wanted.

If schools would learn what children's goals are and how much they vary, instead of setting up goals that they assume all children *should* want to reach, they would begin to discover how to teach, for they would come to understand how children learn.

An example from my counselling experience will serve. A university student came in and told me that he was a failure and was in a state of not being able to study at all. Actually, he had passed his first year, but with rather low marks. "My father wants me to be a brilliant student and I'm not." Asked what *he* wanted, he said, "I want to get my degree and go into business." What did he have to do to get his degree? "Pass my examinations."

"Well, you have," I told him. "Each one you passed has been a success because it brought you nearer your goal. Now, what mark do you have to get to pass?"

"Fifty per cent."

"All right," I said, "to get your degree, which is *your* goal, you have to get 50 on each exam. You have enough intelligence to do that. Set 50 as your sub-goals; then each 50 is a success because it brings you nearer your goal. After all, no one in business ever asked a prospective employee about scholarship, only about degrees!" So the young man decided to aim at 50 as a means of working towards *his* goal. Incidentally, he graduated with honours.

Role of Authorities in Decision-Making

Which brings us to the uses of an authority. During the preliminary stage, while one is gathering data upon which to make a decision, one may seek everywhere for material to make the decision more acceptable. When one goes beyond one's own experience, one goes to an authority which may be a book, a demonstration, a friend, a group, a colleague, or an expert. These are authorities and function as dependent agents. They are mature agents if we ask them to tell us what consequences we might expect. They are the sources of factual material. One may give to them the weight they deserve, based on the accuracy of their foresight in the past. If, on the other hand, one goes to someone for "advice" and accepts the advice, then blames the authority if the advice was not sound, he is using the authority as an immature dependent agent. For example, a mature situation might involve the purchase of a house. One goes to an evaluator who points out the advantages and disadvantages of the building but intimates that the choice is up to the purchaser. If the evaluator were to say, "If I were you, I would buy this house," he ceases to be a mature agent and begins to assume some of the responsibility for the purchaser. Such responsibility, of course, he will deny after the purchase, unless he says, "If it doesn't turn out as I say, I will refund the purchase price." Then of course there is really no decision to be made except that of placing yourself in his hands. In a great many cases this kind of "authority" relationship persists between father and son, where the son apparently makes decisions but expects (rightly so, perhaps) to be bailed out when the going gets rough. A young surgeon with a difficult case on his hands consults his senior, who from his own experience gives him the pros and cons. But unless the senior participates in the treatment, he leaves the decision to the junior, who, in turn, operates. Whether he is successful or not he does not blame the senior, nor does the latter take the credit. In this way a junior someday becomes a senior.

Making Consequences Turn Out Right

Making decisions can be fun. There is always tension. Gathering material for more major decisions constitutes research. The feeling of accomplishment that accompanies the final push can be exhilarating and at the same time relaxing. The tough part is making the decisions come "true." How easy it used to be to end the story, "and they lived happily ever afterward." On the other hand this solution was far more courageous than the present-day tendency of novelists to leave everything up in the air and let the readers act as immature dependent agents.

The consequences following a decision are more difficult to study. One can never predict with 100 per cent success what the events after a decision will be. Unexpected things may happen no matter how much forethought is used. What *is* important is to follow the decisions with actions that make the decision turn out right.

Let us look at the following situation in which the choosing of one of two alternatives is difficult because the anticipated consequences seem to be of equal value. Let us assume that the president of a railroad must decide whether to run a line through district A or district B. In each district is a small town equally populated and prosperous. After getting all the information from his staff and advice from his directors, the choice still remains equivalent. And facetiously he thinks, "I might just as well toss a coin!" As a matter of fact, he is quite right. One of the paradoxes of decision-making is that the more difficult it is to make a decision (that is, the more nearly the possible consequences balance each other), the less it matters which choice is made, because it is what happens *afterwards* that determines the efficacy of the choice. To return to our railroad president: suppose he tosses a coin and the line goes through A. Immediately, through the various forms of advertising, through public relations and the exploitation of land and industrial potential, district A increases in population, the village grows into a town, land values increase, and prosperity grows. District B suffers somewhat from the rivalry and in the course of a decade it can be said, "The president certainly made the right choice. Look what would have happened if he had chosen district B." (Of course, if in the centre of district B they subsequently discovered oil, he would have been criticized for making the "wrong choice," though there would have been no evidence of this when the choice was made.) And so it is with choosing a career, a home, a spouse, a stock, a friend. What a person does to justify his choice is the important thing. That is, to a large extent the individual has the opportunity to make his choices turn out "right": to determine the consequences. If they do not so turn out because of factors outside of his control, he must cut his losses and charge it up to experience. It is thus that we improve our judgment. How often do we ascribe "luck" to someone who has seen to it that his choices are *made to be right*? "Lucky" is the term we apply to the other fellow who was ready at the time to make a quick decision, willing to accept the consequences, and who then did his utmost to make the consequences acceptable.

11 · The Scope of the Security Theory

In which security is shown to be an all-inclusive and all-pervasive concept; in which security patterns are shown to develop and vary in different life-areas; in which the implications of the Security Theory for counselling and education are explored.

THE CONCEPT of security is all-inclusive and all-pervasive. By "all-inclusive" I mean that all aspects of an individual's behaviour in all areas of his life can be interpreted in terms of security. By "all-pervasive" I mean that the actions of all individuals in all places and at all times can be viewed in the scheme of security theory. This does not mean that security is to be considered a panacea for all the world's ills, or as a new form of religion. It is a system of psychology which meets the criteria of being both comprehensive and consistent.

It is not inappropriate to review briefly the main tenets of the security system, as they were outlined at the annual meeting of the Canadian Psychological Association in 1958 and reproduced in the article in the *Canadian Journal of Psychology* quoted in the last chapter. The remainder of this section is from the article.

Security is a state of mind in which one is willing to accept the consequences of one's behaviour. From this starting point, one can envisage an infant, at first wholly dependent upon an agent, feeling secure because the agent is responsible for his decisions. This is *immature dependent security*. [See Chart IX.] From this state he gradually emerges into a state of insecurity, and hence anxiety, from which he can extricate himself, if he so wishes, in one of four ways: first, by reverting to the state of immature dependent security, a regressive mechanism which is wholly salutary in infancy and depends for its efficacy upon the adequacy of the "immature agent" (usually

CHART IX

DIAGRAM OF SECURITY DEVELOPMENT

SECURITY MODEL

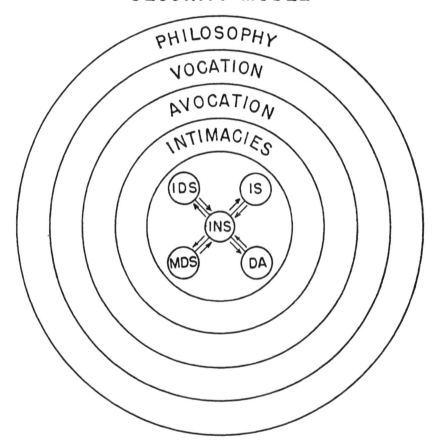

IDS: immature dependent security; INS: insecurity;
IS: independent security; MDS: mature dependent
security; DA: deputy agents.

the parent); secondly, through a process of expending effort, he may learn, acquire knowledge, accept consequences, and hence becomes *independently secure*; thirdly, to bolster up his inadequacy (which is the gap between his own knowledge and omniscience), he may acquire a "mature agent" in terms of an intimate outside his family who serves in lieu of the "immature agents" from whom he has emancipated himself; this is *mature dependent security*. The fourth device for avoiding insecurity is to employ a *deputy agent*. These agents are the behaviour patterns that have been called neurotic. They encompass all those mechanisms which are listed under psychopathological signs—hysteria, mania, paranoia, etc.

It is suggested . . . that these deputy agents are manifest in all children (as can be readily observed); that as the child grows up he learns to lean on some which he has considered successful in dealing with his insecure states; and that all adults manifest in times of crisis or semi-crisis their chosen deputy agents, which in turn become more and more automatized. It is further suggested that mental illness is the pattern of behaviour that an individual manifests when he has succumbed to these devices for dealing with insecurity, instead of acquiring independent security or mature dependent security. Mental illness is a generic term, and is not made up of the specific disease entities included in the psychiatric nosology.

Furthermore, with this security model in mind, it can be seen that the growing child develops patterns of security and dependency first in the area of intimacies, in the family, and later outside it. At about four or five, his interests begin to solidify (avocation); then, at eight or nine, he has more or less accepted the routine requirements of an environment (vocation); and finally, after nine (mental age), he begins to acquire a philosophy in which the concept of purpose first emerges.

All-Inclusive Aspect of Security

Let us return to the ideas that security is all-inclusive and all-pervasive. Developmentally the four areas, intimacies, avocation, vocation, and philosophy, appear in chronological sequence. In the adult, however, these four together with possibly additional areas or sub-divisions of areas make up the sphere of life action. He is involved in social relations, in familial and extra-familial intimacies, or in groups of an immediate or community nature; or he is engaged in such interests as his hobbies and his job or profession; or he is concerned with action in terms of his code, his ideas of authority and justice, or his prevailing sense of purpose in life. Every individual can be studied to ascertain what form of security he is using or what his state of insecurity is in each of these areas. It is by no means the same for all people. One person may use a high degree of independent security in his vocation, but be filled with great insecurity in his extra-curricular life. Another may be immaturely dependent in his intimacies but at least assume a high degree of skill and knowledge in his job. The use of deputy agents, of course, is greatest in those areas in which the individual feels most insecure. Thus, we find an individual who uses the deputy of constantly blaming his employer because he can avoid the consequences of having done so, while on the other hand he rarely blames his parents or his friends for his lack of success. It is rare to find an individual who has achieved a secure solution in each of these areas and in every aspect of his life. However, a high degree of insecurity in one area, if left unsolved, may progressively spread into other areas and eventually permeate all aspects of the individual's life. The sad result is the incapacitated mental patient who is completely helpless and has completely regressed, for whom rehabilitation is a long and arduous process—if it can ever be accomplished. On the other hand, whether frequent use of security solutions in one area, say vocation, can compensate for lack of such solutions in other areas is an open question.

All-Pervasive Aspect of Security

When I refer to security as being all-pervasive, I mean that the actions of all people can be interpreted in its terms. The retarded and the bright child or adult, the handicapped or the highly skilled, the delinquent and the leader, the conforming and the creative, can all be viewed in security terms. So can the workman or the professor, the physician or the politician, the hobo or the president. It would be a good exercise if the reader could take some of the public figures who appear in our press or on our TV screens and attempt to analyse their actions in security terms—especially those who make such a nuisance of themselves and impede constructive action.

I do not want to use any current examples but the whole spread of bureaucracy, not only in governments, but in all other organizations, is based on substitution of deputy agents such as "passing the buck" for the straightforward efforts which follow independent or maturely dependent lines. As officials and committees within the bureaucracy hide behind a screen of anonymity, their action is also a form of regression. Secrets are for the eight-year-olds who because of their lack of independence or mature dependency find safety in the anonymity of actions which a chosen few share. When grown-ups fall back on this device, it reflects the general immaturity of our society because it becomes a means of avoiding consequences. We must, of course, distinguish between secrecy and respect for confidential matters. The latter is necessary in all societies we can visualize. In a truly mature society we might imagine that there would be no need for either—for all human action would be respected and accepted.

The all-pervasive nature of security applies by inference to *all* societies, not merely our own. I know little of other societies (especially the so-called primitive ones) except what I read in books whose veracity may often be questioned; so, unlike some of my psychological colleagues who are prone to jump in where anthropologists fear to tread, I hesitate to say much about the security patterns of the south sea islanders or the North American Indians. Let him who wishes, do so. I expect he would find that the life-areas differ and that some forms of security and some particular deputy agents are more acceptable and, therefore, more frequently used in some societies than in others.

Again, it would be possible to interpret historical and literary figures in terms of the security theory. Indeed I have had considerable pleasure in latter years in doing so as a form of avocation. Think of Samuel Pepys, Shakespeare, Anthony Trollope, or even Queen Victoria interpetreted in terms of security. How much more interesting than the prevalent psychoanalytic interpretations!

One can speculate further: are wars caused by the clash of the insecurities of individual men? Is the rise of the welfare state an attempt to escape the unfamiliar, frightening novelty of the space and nuclear age by a regression to a state of immature dependence? Is the example of a parliament spending months debating an abstract symbol, such as a new flag, a display of the use of deputy agents by which the necessity of forcing real issues is avoided? I have thought of these and many other similar matters. So far there is no real evidence; perhaps another generation will pursue the leads of such speculation.

Implications in Clinical Work

There are two practical aspects of life in which I have applied the security theory and found it not entirely unsuccessful; my clinical work and my plan of education.

No clinician can assess accurately how successful his work has been. Estimates based on a comparison of control groups (that is people with similar difficulties who did not receive treatment) are notoriously unreliable, and counting the number of clients who recovered or improved is no criterion; they might have done so anyhow! Many pathological states are self-limiting.

Nevertheless, I have found it useful to try to discover in what areas of life a person who comes to me with a problem is using his independent or mature dependent security successfully; to ascertain his established deputy agents (which have often served him up to a point of crisis); to find out where development has become fixated or when he has regressed to immature dependency, and from an analysis of all these to get at the source of his insecurity—which was the underlying cause of his coming to me in the first place.

Remember, insecurity occurs when a person either cannot make a decision or is not accepting a consequence. Depending on the extent to which the person has insight, the main task of the clinician is to clarify the alternatives, forecast the possible consequences of each, and leave it to the individual to decide and to act on his own decision. If the individual capitalizes on the independence and mature dependence he already has, his ability to decide and to act can be strengthened.

Of course, the whole gamut of illnesses found in the psychiatric literature—hypochondria, depression, delusions, etc., as we have already indicated—are in this system outcomes of unwillingness to decide and/or to accept the consequences. They indicate the failure to use independent or maturely dependent solutions.

I have been accused of over-simplication. Yet I have found that the human being is an extremely complex and often bewildering, but always interesting creature. The Security Theory has been misinterpreted by some as a method of pigeon-holing man's varied and complicated activities. This it is not; rather it is a system by which man's potentialities can be clarified not only to the clinician but to the individual himself. However, insight in itself is not enough. Indeed, continual talk, as advocated in some systems of therapy, may become a deputy agent. The patient goes on talking about himself until he arrives at a conclusion that his present difficulty in getting along with his employer is due to the fact that his mother rejected him when he was six months old and, therefore, he can excuse himself for anything. This is not insight—it's putting on a pair of blinkers to avoid what he really has to deal with now. In my system insight means that the person becomes aware of what types of security action he is actually using. He comes to know his deputy agents and regressions, but he also gains understanding of what independent and mature dependent security he has and how he may use it more effectively. I hope elsewhere to report more fully on the use of security as a clinical technique and to describe some of the many cases in which it has been used.

Implications for Education

Education is far more important than therapy and ideally should make the latter unnecessary. All children in our society, whether they want to or not, go to school for about half their waking hours for at least ten years of their lives. The school is potentially the most powerful community institution there has ever been for the promotion of mental health. Making decisions and accepting the consequences is a matter of learning and it is this learning which should be the core and basis of all curricula. Despite the hours of debate, it really matters very little what "subjects" make up a curricula. Except for the basic skills—the three R's—required for living in our society, it makes little difference whether history is taught for three hours and flute-playing for one. What does matter is the security patterns the child is learning to use. Is he learning to make decisions and accept the consequences of them? Is he learning that failure is an inevitable part of learning and is not reprehensible? Is he learning that it is the achieving, not the achievement that matters? That achievement is simply a stepping-stone to continuing effort towards further achieving? In our own school we attempt to demonstrate that these things can be. To teachers who take our courses, we show that in a classroom designed to promote mental health and respect for individual differences, the need for competition is eliminated; that the quick or early acquisition of a skill is not nearly as important as the development of interest that will mature further and foster continued effort. We are not as concerned about whether a child reads at three or at seven, but rather whether he is interested in reading, whether he will continue to use reading intelligently as an adult, whether it will be a solace in his old age.

There is a great deal of money being poured into education nowadays. Teachers are well paid, buildings involve a capital investment of millions of dollars, wise men spend a great deal of time revising curricula, planning programmes for enrichment for the slow learner, for the handicapped, and so on. If one-tenth of this amount were directed toward educating teachers, principals, and administrators in an understanding of human development and the ways and means of promoting mental health, one-half of our mental institutions could be closed down in another generation. I have always considered that the teaching of teachers is one of the most important things we do at the Institute. I have described in the Bulletin of the Institute of Child Study something of what we teach our teachers:

A good teacher must know what he teaches: if he is teaching chemistry, he must know chemistry. But his teaching will be ineffectual, and indeed detrimental, unless he knows a good deal about *whom* he is teaching. The learner is an active creature who grows according to laws which are beginning to be well known. Insofar as it is possible to develop education on the laws of human development, we are going in the right direction. As an Institute of Child Study, we see ourselves as a centre whose purpose it is to demonstrate some of the ways in which this can be done, and to try continually to do it better. If the knowledge we gain from our search cannot be applied in our own schools, to our staff, among ourselves, it is of little value. We fail many times, not always because we do not know enough, but because we do not know how to apply our knowledge in a busy organization that is moving on apace. We certainly have not found an educational system that is perfect, nor can we advise others to follow the identical ways that we have found to be satisfactory. Here, however, are a few of the established facts about human living and the ways in which we have attempted to incorporate them into our schools.

Fear is known to be the most dangerous form of motivation, not because it is ineffective but because it is too effective. Chronic fear is like a low-grade infection, continually lowering the mental health level of an individual. So we have eradicated fear from our classrooms. As competition can too easily become a form of fear, we have set out to eliminate it from all parts of our programme except in games, where it legitimately belongs. No threats, no sarcasm, no feeling that the teacher will like a child less if he does not get his work done, no suggestion that he is not as good as the next child because his voice is not as true. This does not mean that fear never enters life at the school; of course it does, for fear is a part of all life. But we do not add deliberately to what life itself has already provided.

As a substitute for the indiscriminate use of fear under the guise of competition, a modern successful teacher uses her knowledge of the mechanism of learning as a guidepost. Research in "learning" marches apace and there are many theories concerning its detailed qualities, characteristics, and functioning. However, it is generally agreed that there are at least three aspects of learning which are of paramount importance to the teacher: *motivation, capacity and persistence*. In simple language, a child will learn when he wants to, when he is capable, and if he puts forth effort.

Motivation

There are at least two faces to this aspect of learning: *interest* and *consequences*, the former inherent, the latter added to the situation by the teacher.

Interest. It is quite obvious that children learn when they are not in school. At cottage or camp or home, they do learn. In fact, it is only in school that it has been necessary to introduce fear to make children learn. Taking a hint from the non-school area, we have come to see that a child in an environment rich in ideas and materials cannot be kept from learning. If a child feels that a teacher genuinely wants to help him learn, he will submit to the necessary drills, the routines, the tedious task, as part of the wise proceedings. Such a teacher is said to be inspiring.

Consequences. But the choice as to whether the child will learn or not is left to *him*. It is *his* decision to learn, not ours to *make* him learn. If he is obstreperous and disturbing, he has obviously chosen not to learn. The consequence of such a choice is that as the classroom is a place for people who want to learn, he will have to go off by himself where he will not disturb others. We do not beg him to come back, nor do we despise him if he stays away. The fact is that he soon *does* come back, because to learn is far more interesting than not to learn. The classroom is far more interesting and exciting than being alone.

Capacity

Children are not all the same. They differ in intelligence, in speed of learning, in personality, in various aptitudes. The fact of individual differences is basic to all teaching.

The basis for the class grouping at the Institute is chronological age; the age spread within a classroom is one year, and a class is limited to twenty or twenty-five children. Having thus ruled out differences of age, we expect our teachers to be able to consider variation among children, and to encourage each according to his capacity and motivating impulses. At the same time the teacher may show that the classroom is enriched by differences in personality; that every child, from the shy to the most aggressive, from the most athletic to the most artistic, has some contribution to make by which the group is enriched. The appreciation among children of each other's differences rather than of each other's similarity is a basis for the establishment of most of the human virtues: tolerance, understanding, consideration, and appreciation.

Persistence

The most pressing problem today, as it apparently has always been, is how to get a pupil to "work." How often does a distracted teacher write on a report card, "Could do better work if he would only apply himself"? Of course he could! But how do we get him to do so? You can lead a youth to culture but you can't make him think!

Bribery, coercion, persuasion, diversion, have all been used, often to no avail. There is only one device that inevitably will function effectively, and that is the development of a feeling of satisfaction in a task well done, the expenditure of effort, not for its own sake (this is the cult of perspiration) but to get somewhere, or something, at some time. We must begin early to preserve this psychological phenomenon which can be observed in all infants. The use of artificial incentives, such as prizes, rewards, honours, medals, stultifies this experience because *these* then become the desired end and, if missed, cause the despair and disappointment of failure. Failure can and should be the spur to *greater* endeavour. The attitude towards failure is the basis of a system of values. We want our children to ask, "Is what I'm working for worth the effort?" rather than, "What does it cost?" or "What will people think?" or, "What prestige will it give me?"

Some teachers are able to foster, encourage, and strengthen this propensity in children for effort towards a goal. Once lost it is difficult to reinstate.

That is why the elementary school is so important—not for the curricular content nor for the excellence of performance but rather for the preserving of a pupil's ability for sustained effort towards a meaningful goal. Given this trait, we need not worry too much about the others. Such a pupil will go forward to significant and outstanding accomplishment in *his* chosen field. He may not do well at examination. But usually he has enough understanding to pass.

A teacher who gives the pupils the feeling that he *wants* them to learn, who appears unperturbed by honest mistakes, who approves of experimentation, can strengthen this feeling of satisfaction in his class. The children feel that he is with them, not against them, that he is a helper rather than a faultfinder. Even in the university system a great many students think that the professors are doing their best to "pluck" them. Such an idea must have arisen in the atmosphere of learning in which they grew up.

The basic task of every school system in our western civilization has been to help teach children those skills which are necessary to our way of life. Our way of life is based on "word" and "number"; hence some skill in reading and writing and numbers is an essential requirement in schooling. Both conservative and progressive schools include these in their curricula; so do we at the Institute. The methods by which these subjects have been taught have been investigated and evaluated continually in all educational circles. We know that children progress in these subjects at different rates, that they are ready for them at different times, that the earliest reader is not necessarily the best, that the quickest reader is not necessarily the one who enjoys the world of literature most. Hence we have learned that a teacher must be concerned with Johnny's progress in terms of Johnny, and not in terms of how he compares with the other pupils. Also, we have learned to think of the three R's not as ends in themselves, but as means, as tools for a job. The level a child has reached in reading is not as important as his confidence in books, his enjoyment of words, his use of these in tasks he encounters, and his dawning awareness that through them he can open the door to the vast world of human thought.

But however confident we feel that we have learned *some* of the facts about learning and teaching, we know that there is a far larger area about which we know little. We would like to ask a few questions for which the answers are still nebulous or lacking. We would suggest that anyone who does *not* know the answers should not be too dogmatic about what should be done about education.

At each age what is the appropriate size of class for the most effective teaching? At what age in an individual's development should various subjects, such as reading, algebra, calculus, economics, music, be introduced into a formal classroom? Should all children, irrespective of capacity, be expected to learn to read, to write, to multiply? If the criterion of selection is not capacity, what should it be? Should there be enriched, accelerated, or restricted curricula? Is the modern high school curriculum based on vocational, avocational, social, or TV requirements? Should teachers be paid less than, more than, or the same as equally capable workers in industry? Should education be wholly free from nursery school to graduate school? Should schools be responsible for moral, aesthetic, and ethical standards as well as intellectual training? Are teachers, artists, singers, surgeons, born or made?

The list could be extended. The interesting fact about these questions is that many people have opinions about them, but few have facts with which to answer them. That education will continue to progress is assured, provided that we remain courageous enough to ask such questions and sufficiently stubborn to insist on discovering more facts with which to supply their answers.

And so we return to our beginning. "Consciousness is the stuff we use to get what we want. We select our goals and we decide on the actions we will take to reach them. If we are willing to accept the consequences of our actions, our state of mind is said to be secure. The feeling accompanying this state may be called serenity, which is the basic goal of all living beings."

Postscript • MARY L. NORTHWAY

STUDENTS frequently referred to the security theory as "the gospel according to Blatz," and colleagues vehemently challenged his postulates and on occasion strengthened their own studies through their desire to prove him wrong. Yet for Blatz security was no gospel to be accepted as dogma. He expected his expositions on security to provoke questions and to stimulate research. They did. This postscript contains some of the recurring questions which the theory aroused, some of Blatz's answers to them, and a summary of the studies and publications which emerged from the interchange.

Although the questions often appeared in superficial and trivial forms, they were concerned with vital issues which neither philosophers nor psychologists have fully resolved. I have tried here to put them in the form in which they actually appeared, and to deal with those which most frequently recurred.

SECURITY AND ETHICS. *If security means making decisions and accepting the consequences, is a man who decides to commit murder and is quite willing to be hanged or suicide and is quite willing to be dead, to be considered secure?*

Blatz's answers to this varied on different occasions. One was that all decisions do not reflect security, and one may sometimes choose a deputy. A man with a high degree of independent security would not commit murder. Murder, like many other antisocial acts, is committed because the murderer perceives the other person as blocking his goal and therefore decides to do away with him. If the murderer were independently secure, he would expend effort to find other routes by which he could circumvent the blocking object and attain his goal. Suicide is a complicated matter, but it may be thought of as the final decision emerging from complete insecurity, and resulting in freedom from having to make any further decisions, a freedom achieved by final withdrawal of one's self.

On other occasions Blatz said, "Security theory is tenable only within a system of ethics, and in a society which has moral limits. Killing or harming others or one's self deliberately are beyond these limits." This thesis is discussed in chapter 7, in which one of the qualities of independent security is shown to be the willingness to accept authority. "An individual seldom resorts to force if he is independently secure."

THE MEANING OF SERENITY. Students and younger staff members frequently asked, *Is serenity really the chief end of life? Who wants to be serene?* In our sessions with the tape recorder, Blatz and I looked up *serenity* both in the dictionary and in *Bartlett* and listed its meanings and usages, such as,

> But an old age serene and bright
> And lovely as a Lapland night,
> Should lead thee to thy grave.
>
> —Wordsworth

and

> Serene, I fold my hands and wait,
> Nor care for wind, nor tide, nor sea.
> I rave no more against time or fate
> For lo! my own shall come to me.
>
> —Burroughs

Blatz agreed that such quotations did not represent his use of *serenity*. It was no "Calm of mind, all passion spent." Rather he meant to imply an equanimity; the third definition in the Oxford dictionary, "of a person, his mind, etc.: calm, tranquil, untroubled, unperturbed," approximates his meaning. Two expressions which he used frequently— to the troubled person, "It will be all right," and in an agitated situation, "tout s'arrangera"—reflect the meaning he attached to *serenity*. I never heard him actually define it, but I do recall him saying in a staff discussion, "If any of you can think of a better English word, we will use it."

SECURITY AND LAISSEZ-FAIRE ATTITUDE. *Does the Security Theory imply a laissez-faire attitude?* The emphasis on the acceptance of consequences suggests the acceptance of the *status quo*, the ideal community being made up of "lotus eaters" entertaining a philosophy of "what will be, will be." All who knew Blatz personally were well aware that this attitude was the antithesis of his own way of life. He never accepted the *status quo* in education or in child care, nor did he bend to prevailing winds of psychological theory or research.

His answer to this query was that an individual accepts the consequences of *his own* decisions, not those of other people. Therefore, if he perceives injustice in a powerful administration, he does not comply. Rather he decides how to go about rectifying the problem, and he accepts the resulting consequences—ostracism, loss of job or prestige—as they come to him. But Blatz also stated that direct attack on injustices in social matters was in itself not enough. "The individual has to decide what the most effective method is to attain the long-term goal which he considers desirable and he has to use his independent skills with patience and wisdom to reach it." Blatz was no agitator. He had little use for the impetuous frontal attack which he felt often did more harm than good by arousing men's anger and "deputy agents." "The main thing is persistence, and few people have enough of it. It may take years to effect changes we feel desirable. It is the continuation of effort steadily in the one direction that matters. We often have to do this, and sometimes we have to retreat in order to advance." At this time it is not inappropriate to say that his own life effort—building the Institute of Child Study—exemplifies his approach to the use of security theory in effecting change in the *status quo*. His persistence in the longitudinal method of research also demonstrates his belief that effective change is a long-term matter. "We must not give up long-term goals for short-term gains."

DECISION-MAKING. Blatz was often considered over-rational. The question was frequently asked, *Suppose I do make a decision and am quite definite about it. But I continue to worry, or to be restless or discontented. How is this explained?* His answers were two. One was that the person had not really made a decision but was still considering an alternative. The second was that a decision is not completed until action is taken on it and the consequence is found satisfactory and therefore accepted. Whether these answers will satisfy the reader to a greater extent than they did many of his discussants remains to be seen.

MAN AND SOCIETY. Many people questioned Blatz's views of man in society, and it was here that he and I differed continually. Blatz's views on social relationships are given in the text. These, as mentioned in the preface, are his later views, in which the importance attached to mature dependence in interpersonal relationships increased. Yet Blatz was never concerned with human social organization, structure, and movement as such. He termed the social sciences "fuzzy." He interpreted all history as a series of decisions made by individuals over time, and he reduced social movement to a complex of the decisions made by each of the persons involved.

A reference which he made to my own interest in sociometry made his point of view clear to me. He said: "But, of course, there is nothing in your studies that does not fit my security theory. All you do is to ask each individual to make a decision about who he likes to play with, and so on. His reply is a decision based on his independent security. Of course, if *you* want to put all the decisions of the individuals together and make up your diagrams that is perfectly legitimate, but remember, all you have is the sum of decisions made by individuals. That is all there can ever be in any social situation no matter what the social psychologists say."

In this way he reduced the areas of communication, social structures, and group processes in security theory to individual decisions. Blatz wholeheartedly maintained that "men shape events, not events, men." Nevertheless, the importance he attached to direct interpersonal relationships cannot be over-emphasized. It stands out in this book perhaps only less strongly than it did in his life.

It may well be that by excluding the wider social matters from his theory, Blatz reflected the fact that he paid little attention to them in his own life. His life at the Institute (and possibly elsewhere) was based on a one-to-one relationship with each member of his staff and with each child in his school. Organizations, committees, etc. were both unnecessary and irksome to him. He was not a joiner, though he enjoyed groups. But social groups to him were the individuals who made them up. It was individuals whom he enjoyed, and from whom he gained his knowledge.

That Blatz was and remained an individualistic psychologist is not surprising. As a psychologist and a physician, his primary view of the human being was in terms of his biological functioning. Energy was basically channelled through the six physiological appetites, the emotions, and the movements of approach and withdrawal (the attitudes); all of behaviour and experience must be reduced to these. From this beginning, Blatz gradually evolved his system in which wants and goals overshadowed needs, and conscious experience became more important than physiological events.

SECURITY IN RELATION TO OTHER PSYCHOLOGICAL SYSTEMS AND TRENDS. Blatz was frequently asked, especially by his more mature colleagues, how he viewed his theory in relation to other systems and schools. His answers were usually elusive, and I can only repeat what I remember him most consistently saying. He often mentioned the positive influence of his teacher, Harvey Carr, whose theory of sensory consequences, as it relates to learning, is reflected in Blatz's security system. He also referred to the fact that as a young man he had read the entire works of Freud (possibly encouraged somewhat by the fact that psychoanalysis was at the time almost unmentionable on the Toronto campus) and had set forth to prove him wrong. Blatz fought youthful, dramatic battles with the Freudians, and continued his sorties and marches into psychoanalytic territory throughout his life. The influence of the school of psychoanalysis was to motivate him to say the opposite of what the Freudians held. He was concerned with mens future, rather than their past; their possibilities, rather than their problems; with what they could make happen, rather than what had happened to them. He stated that long-term psychoanalytic therapy could become a deputy agent by which an individual could by talk conveniently escape dealing with matters he should be facing. Yet he always supported his colleagues who chose to carry out or undergo this form of therapy.

Many of his students and colleagues have seen a similarity between psychoanalysis and security, and have pointed out the resemblance between the unconscious and the underlying processes of which the individual is unwitting; the id and the physiological appetites, the independent acceptance of a code and the super-ego, the deputy agents and the defence mechanisms. But it would be quite inaccurate to suggest that Blatz accepted any such perceived similarities. He remained opposed to psychoanalytic theory throughout his life.

Blatz never attempted to give the chapter and verse of his sources. In his lectures or writing he rarely quoted other people; when he quoted, he quoted Blatz. Yet this was not because he was unaware of what was going on in the psychological field. He knew a great many outstanding scientists locally and internationally in the psychological, psychiatric, mental-health, and educational areas. He communicated with them and assimilated ideas from them. But he continually sifted their ideas into his own system. He deplored the prevailing tendency of attaching hundreds of references in theses and books, for he considered it a form of prestige-seeking—"the game of names." "Why can't a man say what he has to say without bolstering his argument by a lot of references?"

Yet Blatz read widely to keep up with the scientific and professional literature. He was well aware of trends, schools, discoveries, and conflicts among the scholars. But his reading was wider than these, and as he became older he concentrated on novels, history, biography, essays, diaries, often detective stories, but never poetry. He became disappointed with the publications from the psychological scientific establishment, which he thought emphasized design rather than purpose, and preferred rigid experimentalism and statistical manipulation *per se* to a genuine search for knowledge. Yet he viewed the withdrawal into the ivory lab as a temporary and perhaps necessary phase of psychological science. "It is a phase, and clever men are caught by it. This too will pass; we may be better for it."

My own impression is that Blatz's failure or inability to define his sources show that they were too wide to be cited from psychological, scholarly, and scientific writings. Indeed, all of life was his psychological laboratory, from his knowledge of children at play to his observations of scientists caught in the web of fashionable scientific effort. He read the learned books, but he weighed them against the view from his window of children on the playground; he knew his psychiatric nosology, but he balanced it against the problems of his youngest staff member in distress; he participated in the administrative problems of introducing and building a new faculty within an old, great, and established university, but he balanced this difficulty against his own enjoyment of his grandsons, to whom he has dedicated this book. All of this, including his observations of the cattle on his farm and of the behaviour of scholars at scientific conferences, made up his data as a psychologist. He trusted his own judgment to weigh the relative importance of what he read in scientific papers and scholarly books with what he learned from the villagers in Caledon East and what he discovered from his many friends in financial, industrial, governmental, and other areas of life. This encompassing viewpoint is not *à la mode* at present. To express it in a little book without documentation is not in keeping with the times. Yet Blatz realized that times change, and what is considered a period piece today may be viewed as *avant garde* tomorrow. The important thing was to have faith in one's own wisdom and to give expression to it in the best form one could find.

I do not think this reflects temerity on Blatz's part; rather it epitomizes exactly what he meant by "independent security." That his theoretical thinking was never abstracted too far from immediate human reality may be illustrated by a remark he made in discussing the format of this book during the OFF portion of a tape-recording session. "Remember, a little book will not distract the reader from what I want to tell him, and besides, it is so much more comfortable to hold."

PUBLICATIONS AND STUDIES ON SECURITY

I. EARLY STATEMENTS

SALTER, MARY D. "The Concept of Security as a Basis for the Evaluation of Adjustment." Unpublished Ph.D. Thesis, University of Toronto Library, 1939.
——— "An Evaluation of Adjustment Based on the Concept of Security." *Child Development Series*, #18. Toronto: University of Toronto Press, 1940, pp. 72.
BLATZ, W. E. *Hostages to Peace: Parents and the Children of Democracy*. New York: Morrow, 1940, pp. 208.
——— *Understanding the Young Child*. Toronto: Clarke Irwin & Co., 1944, pp. 278.

II. RESEARCH STUDIES

Ph.D. Theses (University of Toronto Library)

GRAPKO, M. F. "The Relation of Certain Psychological Variables to Security." 1953, pp. 233.
KESCHNER, DOROTHY. "Dependence and Independence in Young Children." 1957, pp. 46 and appendix.

M.A. Theses (University of Toronto Library)

AINSWORTH, L. H. "Rigidity as a Manifestation of Insecurity." 1950, pp. 66.
BLUM, MARY H. "Security of Adolescents in their Use of Money." 1950, pp. 64.
HIRSCH, M. "A Clarification of the Concept of Security in the Academic Area and its Relationship to Feeling Tone of a Group of Grade X Students." 1953, pp. 36.
HUTCHISON, H. C. "A Study in Security: Belongingness, Competition, and Sociometric Status." 1952, pp. 53.
KARRY, EVA. "A Comparison of Delinquents and Non-Delinquents on their Feelings of Security and Insecurity in Familial Area." 1951, pp. 49.
LAIDLAW, R. G. N. "An Analysis of the Method of Evaluating Test Items in the Area of 'Vocational' Security of University Students." 1949, pp. 31.
LAURENCE, MARY W. "A Clarification of the Concept of Security in the Familial Area." 1949, pp. 44.
MACNAMARA, PHOEBE. "Personality Scales: A Study in Methodology." 1951, pp. 65.
TOBIN, S. M. "A Clarification of the Concept of Security in the Vocational Area." 1950, pp. 70.
URQUHART, GERMAINE M. "A Study of Negative Behaviour in Infants." 1950, pp. 68.
WALTER, ONALEE J. "A Clarification of the Concept of Security in the Area of Competition." 1950, pp. 47.
WHITEHOUSE, B. M. "Belongingness: Its Nature and Measurement." 1950, pp. 41.

Diploma Studies (Institute of Child Study Library)

Infancy

KILGOUR, MARY. "Adjustment of Babies in an Institution." 1956.
SUTHERLAND, C. J. "A Study of Mental Health in Infants in a Period of Prolonged
   Distress." 1958.

Preschool

ESTABROOK, E. S.; WILLIAMS, MRS. J. M. T.; and NEWBY, F. "An Examination
   of the Similarities and Differences Between Teachers' and Parents' Reports on
   the Mental Health Assessment Record for Preschoolers." 1961.
FISHER, KAREN. A Study of the Changes in Mental Health Status Scores of New
   Nursery School Children." 1956.
HU, MARRIAN. "A Study Relating Children's Adjustment on the Entrance Records
   to their Acceptance and Refusal of Dependence and Independence on the
   Preschool Mental Health Assessment Form in October of Entrance Year."
   1958.
KENDALL, C. "Studies of the Mental Health of the Preschool Child: A Comparison
   of Acceptance and Refusal of Dependence and Independence at Home and
   at School." 1958.
KENNEDY, L. "An Investigation of Changes in Children's Scores Derived from
   Mental Health Assessment Scale Recorded on Nursery School Children." 1957.
McGARRY, M. "A Study of the Relation of Age and Status (as in First or Second
   Year) to the Mental Health Assessment Scores of Nursery School Children."
   1956.
SHERMAN, NORMA. "Studies Toward the Development of the Institute of Child
   Study Mental Health Assessment Record." 1957.
WAIT, P. and SIMONE, V. C. "A Study of the Relationship Between 1962 Play
   Test Scores and Mental Health Assessment Scores." 1962.

School age

ADAIR, J. W.; GLENNON; STOICHEFF; and THOMSON. "Factors Related to Security
   Measures in School-Age Child." 1956.
BLACKFORD, GORDON S. "Comparison of Accelerated and Non-accelerated Students
   According to Interest Patterns, Reading Ability, and Security Feelings." 1957.
BRIDGMAN, P. E. and PETIT, E. J. "Security and Decision-Making." 1963.
GRANT, W. T. "A Study to Investigate the Elementary School Discipline Problem
   in Relation to Security, Anxiety, and Sociometry." 1963.
HANNINGTON, E. I.; MACDONALD, ETTA; MACDONALD, JOHN; and TREHERNE,
   DAVID A. "The Security, Intelligence, Achievement, and Sociometric Status
   of Children in Park and Blythwood Schools as Related at Two Socio-Economic
   Levels." 1962.
LANGSTAFF, ANNE L. and SHARPE, MRS. D. "Relationship between Reciprocals
   and Security as Measured by I. C. S. Security Test and Sociometric Results."
   1962.
WRIGHT, GRACE. "A Comparison Between Sociometric and Jimmy Test Scores of
   Children at Grade Four to Grade Five Level." 1962.

III. JOURNAL PUBLICATIONS

In the Bulletin of the Institute of Child Study

AINSWORTH, MARY D. "Significance of the Five-Year Programme." 1960, pp. 7–16.
BLATZ, W. E. "Curing and Preventing." 1957, pp. 5–8.
————— "Positive Mental Health." 1957, pp. 1–3.
————— "Security and the School-Age Child." 1952, pp. 1–5.

BROWN, M. "The Child Learns through Consequences." 1955, pp. 9–14.
GRAPKO, M. L. "The Development of Security in Children." 1957, pp. 9–12.
—— "Children's Excuses." 1958, pp. 12–15.
—— "The Significance of Social Expectancy and Achievement." 1960, pp. 7–11.
NORTHWAY, MARY L. "Studies in the Growth of Security." 1959, pp. 1–7.

In Other Journals

AINSWORTH, L. H. "Rigidity, Insecurity and Stress." *J. abnorm. soc. Psychol.* LVI (1958).
BLATZ, W. E. "Decisions." *Canad. J. Psychol.* XII:1 (1958).
BLATZ and LAIDLAW, R. G. N. "A Note on 'Consistency' as a Feature of Security Theory." *Ont. Psychol. Quart.* XII:1 (1959).
GRAPKO, M. F. "The Child and His Development of Security." *Canad. Sch. J.* XXXIV:6 (1956).
—— "Security and Mental Health." *Addictions* XI:2 (1964).
LAIDLAW, R. G. N. "A Note on the Origins and Nature of Blatz's Security Theory." *Merrill Palmer Quart.* VI:1 (1959).

IV. BOOKS

AINSWORTH, M. D. and AINSWORTH, L. H. *Measuring Security in Personal Adjustment.* Toronto: University of Toronto Press (1960), pp. xiv, 98.
DAVIS, CARROLL. *Room to Grow.* (In press.)
FLINT, BETTY M. *The Security of Infants.* Toronto: University of Toronto Press (1959), pp. x, 134.
—— *The Child and the Institution.* Toronto: University of Toronto Press (1966), pp. 162.

V. TESTS

FLINT, BETTY M. "The Infant Security Scale." Unpublished. Institute of Child Study Library.
GRAPKO, M. F. "The Story of Jimmy: Security Test, Grades IV to VIII." Institute of Child Study. Available from the Vocational Guidance Bureau, Ontario College of Education, Toronto.
MILLICHAMP, DOROTHY M. "The Preschool Mental Health Assessment Scale." Unpublished. Institute of Child Study Library.

CANADIAN UNIVERSITY PAPERBOOKS

Related Titles in this Series

9 781442 652033